Quick, Boil Some Water!

The Story of Childbirth In Our Grandmothers' Day

Quick, Boil Some Water!

The Story of Childbirth In Our Grandmothers' Day

Yvonne Barlow

Bookline and Thinker Ltd

Quick, Boil Some Water
The Story of Childbirth In Our Grandmothers' Day

Published by Bookline and Thinker Ltd, 2007
Suite 231, 405 Kings Road, London SW10 0BB
Tel: 0845 116 1476
www.booklinethinker.com
email: editor@booklinethinker.com

British Library Cataloguing-in Publication-Data
Quick, boil some water : the story of childbirth in our grandmothers' day
1. Childbirth - History - 20th century
I. Barlow, Yvonne
618.4'0904
ISBN: 978-0-957695771

Acknowledgements:

To all the women who answered the call, it was a privilege to listen to your story. You taught me to take nothing for granted.

Contents

Introduction

Childbirth, as any granny will tell you, was once a journey into the unknown. Rather than ponder which pushchair to buy or fret over towelling or disposable nappies, previous generations of women worried about what lay ahead. Sex education at school was unknown, and some of those pregnant for the first time had no idea how the baby emerged from their swollen tummy. Medical staff rarely gave explanations and would push and prod with little offer of pain relief let alone sympathy.

Today, we hear stories of over-worked midwives and short-staffed hospitals, but the truth is that childbirth has never been easier.

In Ancient Greece, doctors often refused to take pregnant women as patients because the risk of death was high and too many fatalities could ruin a reputation. Medea, a Greek war maiden, was so turned off pregnancy that she said:

I would rather stand three times in a battle line than give birth to one child.[1]

More than two thousand years later and little had changed. In the 1920s a group of women working for social change used the slogan:

It's four times more dangerous to bear a child as to work in a mine; and mining is man's most dangerous trade.[2]

The main dangers in childbirth are heavy bleeding, infection and obstructed labour. Small women, especially girls who haven't stopped growing, are especially vulnerable to obstructed labour. If the pelvis is too small for an infant to pass through then the birth becomes blocked. Without a Caesarean Section, both the infant and mother can die as contractions overwork in an effort to push the baby out.

Older women who have had many children can suffer a similar fate. After numerous pregnancies, their stomach muscles may be loose and overstretched so that an infant is not tucked into the tight up-down position. As a result, the baby can lounge across the womb in any position and, when labour begins, the infant's shoulder or abdomen sits over the opening of the womb. A child cannot be born naturally in this position and, without a Caesarean Section, both mother and baby face death.

And even after the birth of a healthy infant, there are still dangers. If the afterbirth is not delivered quickly from the womb, its bulk can prevent the womb from deflating. This leaves blood vessels open and dripping like faulty taps. Under these conditions, it doesn't take long for a woman to bleed to death.

Infections can happen in the days following birth. As the womb sheds its bloody waste, the warm moist flow provides a hothouse for germs to grow. Bacteria can be quick to multiply, travel upstream to the womb and pass into the blood stream. Many years ago, when bathing was infrequent and hygiene was lax, this was known as Childbirth Fever and caused untold deaths.

Early interventions

In Medieval times, the Christian church had a biblical explanation for the perils of childbirth. They put the blame firmly on Eve and her misdemeanours in the Garden of Eden. The church decreed that women were the "Sisters of Eve", and the rigours of labour were God's punishment for her sins.

Any effort to relieve women's pain in childbirth was looked at suspiciously. *The better the witch; the better the midwife*, was a damning but popular Medieval saying.[3] To guard against witchcraft the church took charge of maternity care. Midwives had to be licensed by a bishop and swear an oath not to use magic when assisting women through labour.[4]

And pregnant women weren't only advised against witchcraft. In Sunday sermons, churchmen advised them to prepare their shroud in case of death, and special prayers were said so that pregnant women would be delivered through the path ahead. Women close to childbirth were encouraged to confess their sins, and water was kept close at hand for a quick baptism by midwives.[5]

Royal women were given the church's highest prayers as they carried heirs to the throne. But this barely compensated for the fact that these regal women gave birth in rooms thronged with courtiers and churchmen who all felt duty-bound to witness that the newborn babe and heir came truly from the royal womb.

James II, an unpopular 17th century monarch, banished the royal observers from his wife's birth chamber after she became ill. James' wife was Catholic and ministers feared a male child, a future king, would be raised with Catholic sympathies. The ministers became suspicious when they saw a large brass warming pan being carried to and from the queen's chamber. When the birth of a healthy son was announced, the ministers accused the king of swapping infants in the warming pan. Their conviction was so strong that James, along with his wife and child, were forced to flee England.

When Marie Antoinette gave birth for the first time a century later, ministers and court officials crammed into the birth chamber and even jostled for space on top of furniture to get a view. The room became so stuffy that the poor woman fell into a coma due to the lack of air.

Science lends a hand

After centuries of avoiding childbirth, scientific strides in the 17th century gave doctors the confidence to finally enter the childbirth chamber.

To help in difficult births, surgeons developed pincers, or forceps, that could be used to grasp the infant and pull it out from the mother's birth canal. However, some of the instruments were crude and grasped more than the baby. As a result, it was not unusual for women to be left with torn bladders or ripped wombs.

Surgeons, and their inventions, did help many women with difficult births, but letting men into the bed-chamber was not a popular trend among husbands. Many feared that the male doctors might become too intimate with their wives. As a result, doctors were forced to adopt a strict code of behaviour to protect the modesty of their patients. Questions relating to periods, bladder or bowel problems could be asked only through an older female attendant. Vaginal examinations were done during a contraction when the woman would be distracted by pain. Childbirth rooms were kept dimly lit and women's bodies covered by bedcovers at all times. Even the delivery was done under the bedcovers and the doctor was forced to feel his way blindly.

One doctor wrote of his first examination of a labouring woman:

> *Whether it was head or breech, hand or foot, man or monkey, that was defended from my uninstructed finger by distended membranes, I was as uncomfortably ignorant, with all my learning, as the foetus itself that was making all this fuss.*[6]

Working blind made forceps deliveries especially difficult. Inexperienced doctors were never sure which part of a woman's anatomy they had caught in their instruments. Even the cutting of the umbilical cord was done under the bedcovers, and some doctors reported male infants losing their penis.

There are few statistics to show whether doctors actually helped reduce the number of women dying in childbirth. A few physicians suggest they made it worse. Oliver Wendell Holmes, a 19th century obstetrician, accused doctors of spreading infection by carrying instruments from patient to patient and not washing their tools between births.[7] Dr. Holmes pointed out that midwives had fewer cases of infection than doctors because they used materials from the patients' own homes. He charted the story of a doctor who lost three patients after he attended their births with samples of a dead woman's afterbirth in his pocket. The doctor continued to deny he was at fault and was well supported by others in the profession.

But Dr. Holmes was ahead of his time. This was an era when even washing hands between patients would have been considered a bizarre ritual. It wasn't until the 1870s, that Joseph Lister's ideas of germs gained credibility and doctors began cleaning up their act.

The Pain

Alcohol was the traditional anaesthetic but it took a lot of beer or gin to have any effect on long and painful labours. In the 18th century the rich began using opium, but addiction and death were both problems.

Chloroform was the first great stride forward. A small amount was dropped onto a handkerchief and the labouring woman held it against her mouth and nose. As she fell into a sleep, her arm would fall away and she would no longer inhale the fumes. As the drug wore off, she was able to reapply the handkerchief and drift back into unconsciousness. Women seeking a pain-free birth clamoured to try it.

But some doctors weren't keen and refused to offer it saying it loosened women's morals. Dr. George Gream, a royal physician in the 1860s, claimed that women were inclined to use obscene language under chloroform. Another physician, Dr. Tyler Smith said that anaesthesia produced "excitement of sexual passion."[8]

Poor women couldn't afford the medicines, or the doctors who came with them. Instead, they had to make do with alcohol or gripping a knotted sheet that hung from the bedpost.

The 20th Century

In the early part of the 20th century, it is estimated that 17 percent of mothers died in childbirth. A study by the Ministry of Health in the 1920s blamed many of the deaths on poor sanitation, heavy work and Rickets, a bone softening disease caused by poor diet.[9]

Concern over the number of deaths was so high that the government set out regulations on the training of midwives. Many young women took the opportunity to train, and the profession gained credibility.

But to earn a living the newly-trained midwives had to charge for their services. As a result, pregnant women would save up a few shillings so they could pay the midwife to stay with them through labour. A few lucky women also had relatives move in to take care of the house and the other children.

As theories about sanitation and hygiene became more accepted, hospitals became cleaner and the number of deaths from infection began to fall. Wealthier women began to choose to give birth in hospital as they could have 24-hour professional care. However, that professional care came with institutional rules on bed rest, infant feeding and even who could visit and when.

On arrival at hospital, women were told to leave their husbands at the front door. Initial care was often a pubic shave, bath and an enema. Painkillers were strong and swift. Women often remembered little of the spotlessly clean delivery room, sterile gowns and glinting forceps. They also didn't hear their baby's first cry.

Sometimes the sedation proved too strong, and some mothers died due to excessive medication. There were also complaints about the system. In a letter to the *Ladies Home Journal*, one mother wrote:

"They give you drugs, whether you want them or not, and strap you down like an animal."

Dr. Grantly Dick-Read was horrified by the fear and pain he saw among London women in his care.

He believed that fear caused muscular tension, which in turn exacerbated the pain of childbirth. He said that if women were told what was happening to their bodies then this would reduce their tension and ease their pain. He published groundbreaking books, *Natural Childbirth* in 1939 and *Childbirth Without Fear* in 1942, and these were read eagerly by the middle classes.

But for many young women, knowledge of birth was limited. Many had no knowledge of what lay ahead, and elderly midwives tell tales of naïve pregnant women who believed the baby would erupt from their belly button.

World War II made life even more difficult, but it also brought medical advancements that made childbirth safer. Penicillin to treat infections, and improvements in blood transfusions were developed for the battlefield. In 1948, the National Health Service was born bringing free health care to all who needed it.

But women still had little control over what happened to them in pregnancy and labour. Physicians and nurses dictated all care, and patients had little option but to accept it. In addition, the church maintained a strong role in childbirth. For many new mothers their first trip outdoors was to church to give thanks for delivering them safely. Churching, as it was known, was popular until the 1960s.

The women's movement in the 1960s and '70s gave many pregnant women the confidence to demand a voice in childbirth. As women took on careers, they were no longer willing to lie unquestioning as mostly male obstetricians made decisions about this momentous event. Armed with information, they said no to enemas, shaving, medication and instrumental deliveries.

The natural childbirth movement was helped along by the growth of female obstetricians who brought a more empathetic attitude to their practice. In addition, the Patients' Charter, launched by the National Health Service in the 1980s, gave women greater choices in their care. Today, providing medical conditions and staffing rates allow, women can select birth at home, hospital and even in a tub of water.

More importantly, the fear and superstition that once made childbirth a torturous experience has been replaced by joyful anticipation.

The women whose stories are documented in this book went through pregnancy when it was known as 'confinement'. Rather than show pride in their pregnancy, many had to hide all evidence of a bump. Few even discussed their experiences. And no one complained.

"We just had to get on with it. There was no choice," said a woman who raised three children when most working class homes still had outdoor toilets and no hot-water plumbing.

I didn't think about these women when I had my own children. Like many modern women, I expected childbirth to be a pain-free emotional experience. And I was lucky. My labours both went well, and I have two beautiful boys. But I also had the cheek to complain. After my first birth I was hungry and there was not even tea and toast on offer. It was a Sunday evening and all the nurses could offer was ice cream and jelly left over from another patient's meal. I'd worked hard that day and felt terribly let down.

Today we groan about poor maternity leave from work and forget that previous generations of women struggled with outdoor toilets, coal fire heating and, for some, there was a war on.

The War Years

1940-1945

In the early 1940s, men left for war and women battled against shortages. Valuable time was spent queuing at shops for rationed supplies. Meals needed determination to turn a daily allowance of two ounces of meat per person into a nourishing meal, and there was no rest in the evening. Clothing was in short supply, therefore socks needed darned, trousers patched and there were pullovers to knit for the children. And women couldn't forget the cleaning. Coal fires meant that dust and grime had to be scrubbed daily, and there were few appliances to help with the grind. Instead it was heavy hernia-popping work that required muscle power for laundry, sweeping, polishing and for carrying coal from outdoor bunkers to the fireplace and stove.

And it wasn't just the house that needed work. Gardens needed daily care as families depended on home-grown vegetables to supplement the paltry rations. Rabbits became popular and hutches were erected in many yards. But the creatures weren't pets. Instead they had great value as an additional source of meat.

Laundry took advance planning and it could take days as few homes had hot water boilers, and soap was rationed. Many women caught rheumatism in the cold damp outhouses where they did their laundry. Outhouses sometimes had a fireplace where water could be boiled for laundry; otherwise women had to boil water on the kitchen stove. Stubborn stains were soaked in soda overnight to loosen the dirt. A wooden stick was used to stir and pummel the clothes before they were scrubbed on a corrugated washboard. The laundry was rinsed and then steered through a mangle to wring out the excess water.

Drying was dependent on good weather, and a spate of rain could bring misery to many homes as damp clothing and linen were draped over anything that stood still.

Disposable nappies were a distant dream, so mothers washed terry towelling nappies on a daily basis. To make matters worse, plastic to make nappy over-pants was in short supply. Sister Mary, the childcare guru who answered mothers' problems in *The Home Companion* magazine during the 1940s, advised mothers to save babies "macintosh" knickers for visiting or travel.[10] Sister Mary was typical of nurses and midwives of this era as she was probably a spinster. While she had the authority to issue advice, she was unlikely to have ever had a child of her own.

Magazines were popular among new mothers seeking tips on coping in this time of crisis. Everything from furniture to cheese was in short supply. Need a dustpan? Make one from an old biscuit tray advised *The Home Companion.* Use an old pair of scissors to cut one end of the metal tray, drill three holes into the back and screw in a handle cut from an old wooden pole. The magazine promised this bit of joinery would take only 30 minutes.[11]

New pinnies, or aprons, could be made by cutting the collars from men's old shirts, adding a waistband and wearing them back to front, according to one magazine. Need a handbag? Then crochet one, advised *Home Chat* magazine. *Women and Home* told housewives to sew one from old coat material.[12]

In addition to handy quick fixes, this was an era when cleanliness was the measure of a woman. Even the front door step had to be scrubbed, and *The Home Companion* advised women to save on soap rations by scrubbing the steps with sand.[13]

Paraffin was another popular cleaner, especially for baths and toilets. But, according to the *Ladies' Mirror,* one woman burned to death after lighting a cigarette in a bathtub that had not been fully rinsed.[14]

Women were bombarded with handy tips on saving soap. These included using cold tea as a cleanser for grubby finger-marked furniture and for polishing windows and mirrors.[15] Women were also told not to waste metal by buying new curtain rings. A 1940s *Women's Own*, advised women to clean the ones they had in vinegar. Holes in linoleum could be filled with melted wax crayon and then coated with varnish. Similarly, holes in enamel basins could be plugged with rags and painted in enamel.[16]

Coal was a vital component for heating and cooking, and *The Home Companion* had a backbreaking suggestion to make it go further. Save the dust from the coal until you have a bucketful. Add a half-bucket of clay, mix it to a mud pie consistency with water and mould it in flowerpots. When dry it could be burned on the fire.[17]

Countrywomen tell of wrapping dried vegetable peelings in newspaper and coating the package in coal dust then burning it as fuel. Nothing was ever wasted.

While women worked hard, they were also advised to look good when their husbands were home on leave. Stockings were in short supply, but women were told to unhook their front suspenders before kneeling down. This would preserve the stockings from holes and ladders, said *Women's Own.*[18] Trouser wearing was rare at this time, but the *Home Companion* magazine advised unpicking a husband's old trousers to make a 'neat little skirt'. And don't throw out old socks, said *Home Chat* magazine. Instead, slit them down the back and feet, sew a few together and make floor cloths.[19]

Other advice included how to create a new lipstick by scooping out old containers, melting the contents and reforming the mass into an old container.[20]

In addition, old bra straps could be replaced by crocheting a ribbon 12 stitches wide, and the gusset of underwear could be replaced by a crochet patch.[21] And if your underwear couldn't be patched, then all was still not lost. According to *Woman and Home* magazine, you could knit some by following their handy pattern.[22] *The Home Companion* gave advice on using net curtains to make "the daintiest little brassiere".[23]

Ready-made sanitary towels were available in the shops, but they were expensive. As a result, many women made their own and washed them after use.

The war brought social problems and many women turned to the agony aunts for advice:

"Nearly a year ago my husband wired that he was going overseas and that he couldn't see me as he wasn't getting any embarkation leave. He said to write to him c/o the Middle Eastern Command till I heard more and he could give me a permanent address. Although I wrote every week, I never got a reply. A friend advised me to write to the War Office. A few weeks later I got a letter from my husband saying he was back in this country but he couldn't give me his address for some time. He promised he would as soon as they stopped moving him around. He asked me not to write to him in the meantime. I got anxious when a fortnight passed and I still hadn't heard. So I went to the town where the postmark was on his last letter to see if I could find out anything.

I found out plenty.

I found out that he had never been out of the country at all and that he had 'married' another woman.

What should I do? The shock has just about made me mental. But we have two kiddies, and I have to think of them. If I start getting a divorce, it will have to come out about the bigamy and the kiddies' father will be sent to prison."

© IPC Media [24]

A heart-wrenching story, but *Home Companion* Agony Aunt Ruby Ayres told the poor woman to force her husband to tell the truth to the new "wife" so that he could return home. Otherwise, she should be prepared to take action against her husband.

Other problems were caused when children were separated from their parents and evacuated to new families in the country. One woman desperately missed her daughter and wrote to *Home Chat*:

"My daughter is an evacuee down in Devon and is very happy with her foster mother who is the nicest woman in every respect, but for the fact that she seems to have grown jealous of my little girl's love for me. She told me her one great sorrow in life was that she was childless and that my Peggy had brought her tremendous comfort. I am rather afraid she may be trying to influence Peggy against me."

Agony Aunt, Mrs Jim, told her to find another home for her daughter.

"This woman may be exercising too strong an influence over the child so that when she comes home she may be unhappy and restless."

© IPC Media [25]

Children in wartime brought other worries.

"I've met a chap – he's in the army – and I think he is the finest man who ever walked. He's so straight and decent that I'm afraid of him, though. He

has such hard and fast ideas on what is right and wrong.

He wants me to marry him, and I want to say yes. But though I am only a Miss, I have a baby. I am working in a war factory and have the baby boarded out near here so I can see her at weekends. The people who have her are so in love with her that they want to adopt her.

What would you do? I love my baby, and it would break my heart to part with her. But I dare not tell my fiancé about her."

© IPC Media [26]

The agony aunt says that if her fiancé is so straight and decent he will forgive her.

Although the war effort required all childless women to work, pregnant women stopped work immediately, even if their position was firmly behind a desk. Expectant mothers received extra food rations, such as one pint of milk a day rather than half a pint every two days. But there were no extra clothing rations, so few women sacrificed coupons to buy maternity clothes. Instead generously-sized clothes were borrowed from larger friends and family. However, some pregnant women invested in a "maternity belt" that sat loose across the tummy but acted like a sling to support the growing bulge.

Babies' clothes were mostly hand knitted, and infants were dressed in layers for warmth. Homes were cold and draughty, and *The Home Companion*'s Sister Mary advised wrapping a child in three layers of clothing when indoors. This involved a long-sleeved vest that was pinned to the nappy to keep the body warm. Over that, the baby would wear a flannel petticoat or bodice and then a dress or romper suit.[27] With waterproof pants in short supply, wet baby clothes dripped into the laundry basket every few hours.

Cots, prams and other baby paraphernalia were in short supply during the war, and women were forced to share. Equipment was passed on as each infant grew. When cribs weren't available babies often slept in drawers or laundry baskets

Feeding, whether it was from the breast or bottle, was strictly orchestrated by nurses. A baby born in the morning was entitled to two feeds on his first day in the world. The unfortunate bairn who came into the world in the afternoon should be fed only once, according to Sister Mary of *The Home Companion.* Thereafter the child was limited to five feeds spaced four hourly with nothing overnight. Pity the poor infant who woke up during the night or who cried hungrily between feeds. They should have water, said Sister Mary. She also said the last feed should be at 9 pm so the mother could be in bed by 10 pm. This way she could be up early to take care of her husband in the morning.[28]

Like feeding, potty training was a rigorous affair with mothers trained to catch defecations after each feed. Nurse Hale at the *Woman's Own* advised:

"At first he was such a clean baby and because you held him out from birth he had obliged you whenever you did so. But suddenly he may turn from his good way and refuse to do what you ask him. He may go stiff and utterly refuse to sit upon his chamber. Or he may sit upon his chamber and play and make no attempt either to pass water or a motion."[29]

Sympathetically, she advised patience.

Other magazine agony aunts weren't so understanding. A mother writing to *Home Chat* magazine in 1942 asked about weaning her baby who was six months old son and weighed 17 pounds.

Dr. Elizabeth Mudie told her:

"Baby is nearly three pounds overweight... He should have only four feeds now, with the last at 7 pm - after which he should sleep around the clock until 7am. Introduce broth and sieved vegetables at the dinnertime feed... gradually introduce him to brains, roes and raw bone marrow."[30]

Very few women consulted a doctor about their child's ailments. Doctors were expensive, and the National Health Service was still a dream. Instead, women mixed together their own compounds, either on the advice of their mother or from a magazine.

According to Nurse Hale of *Women's Own*, sweat rashes stemming from too much clothing could be treated by dusting a baby's face with a mixture of zinc, starch and boracic powder. Similarly, an allergic rash could be bathed with vinegar and water.[31]

Most births took place at home as it was cheaper and because half the nation's doctors and nurses were in military service leaving hospitals severely understaffed. A hospital birth cost £10 to £20 depending on the facility, while the average man's weekly income in 1943 was £3 18 shillings. Working women sometimes paid into an employers' health care insurance plan to cover maternity care.

But most women paid a few shillings to a midwife who delivered them at home.

In preparation for a home birth, mothers were expected to stockpile a hefty collection of linens. Margaret Staples, a midwife in Norfolk in the 1940s, advised mothers to gather the following:

3 baby nightgowns
3 baby back flannels to swaddle the infant and keep it warm
2 strips of cotton to bind the umbilical cord
3 dozen nappies (often made out of old sheets)
I bottle of Lysol (skin disinfectant similar to Dettol)
3 dozen maternity pads (bought or homemade)
Glycerine (for sore nipples)
Vaseline (for baby's buttocks)
Maternal nightgowns
Safety pins
4 Lemonade bottles filled with boiled water that has cooled (this was considered sterile)
Sanitary belt or tape to hold the pad in place
An old sheet folded and padded with a thick layer of newsprint and baked in a warm oven to kill any bugs. (This protected the bed from blood and other fluids. It had to be large enough to cover the mattress from the women's shoulders to her ankles.)

Spare candles and matches were also needed as there were frequent blackouts during the war. In addition, homes without electricity used paraffin lighting and this often ran out when unattended.

Pregnant women were given telephone numbers for the doctor and midwife, but few homes had telephones and husbands had to take to their bikes when a wife went into labour.

Pain relief was almost non-existent. Most midwives travelled by bike or on foot and couldn't carry the weighty canisters of gas and air. Midwives could offer a mild sedative of chloral hydrate, but this was like treating appendicitis with an aspirin. Grin and bear it, was the order of the day.

Doctors were called out to difficult deliveries, and they often knocked women out with chloroform and then took care of the birth with a pair of forceps they carried in their bag. The mother would wake up when the birth was over to find out whether she had a boy or a girl.

Traditionally, a female relative moved in after the birth. She would care for the other children and maintain the home while the mother recovered. Some wealthier women paid for this help. But during the war, many women took up work in factories or joined the services. As a result, there was a critical shortage of home help. Many mothers were forced out of bed early and returned quickly to their roles as cook, handyman, washerwoman, physician, seamstress and housekeeper.

Dorothy
1940

I had a pretty good first pregnancy. I was just over 5 foot 1 inch and so carried the baby forward and quite high. I was uncomfortable but, being a farmer's wife, I had plenty to do and kept going well until the first niggling pains came along.

My husband drove me the 20 miles to the Radcliffe Maternity Hospital in Oxford.

A staff nurse received me and dismissed my husband. They asked me my religion and I remember saying I was agnostic. The staff nurse left me in no doubt that she disapproved of this. She was not a friendly soul, and I began to feel very apprehensive and lonely.

My pains eased and I was left with backache. The next day there was talk of sending me home but the backache increased. I couldn't sleep that night. The backache was worse and I walked around the ward. A nurse saw me and told me to get back to bed.

The next day, I overheard two nurses talking about the bluebells they'd seen on a climb in the hills. This made me feel homesick for the countryside, and I began to cry and shake. They gave me extra blankets and a hot water bottle, but a staff nurse told me I was feeling sorry for myself - I was!

The pain in my back grew worse and I had another sleepless night. My husband came to see me, but I didn't want to see him as I was in so much pain. When he'd gone, I turned onto my knees with my bottom in the air. This eased the backache and amused the other patients - although I was passed caring. I just wanted it to end.

On the fourth day, desperate for some progress, I deliberately wet the bed and told the nurse my waters had broken. They rushed me to the labour ward, and I was examined by a Dr. Balliol.

"Like the college?" I asked him, and he smiled.

In examining me, he broke my waters. The staff nurse was very annoyed with me, but now at least my pains began in earnest. I was left a short while and examined again. Someone said they could see the baby's head. After a lot of pushing and struggling on my part, they put me to sleep.

This was in the late evening and, when I came to in the early hours of the morning, the night sister told me I had a boy. I was thrilled to bits. I was also very sore and could hardly sit up. They gave me a rubber ring to sit on, and my baby was brought in to feed not long after that.

He had a very pointed head because of the forceps that were used to pull him out, but it became more normal after a few weeks.

The doctor later explained that the baby had been facing the wrong way and pressing on my spine all this time. He also said I had a great many stitches. I felt as though someone had twisted all my tenderest parts. It took at least three months before I could go to the lavatory in comfort.

Babies were taken away from their mothers and kept in a baby ward. They were only brought out for feeding. Patrick was a bonnie boy. Later he suffered from migraine and I often wonder if it had anything to do with the forceps delivery.

During my second birth, I heard the doctor tell the nurse he was shocked at the state of my undercarriage. This baby was also facing the wrong way, but my doctor spotted this early on and my labour was at home with my good local doctor and district nurse in attendance. This birth was over in six hours.

Dora
1941

I was 25 and my husband was in the forces. I paid around £20 for a two-week stay at a quality nursing home and lived with my in-laws as my time grew near. I was three weeks overdue when I was rushed down the road in a wheelchair. All through the night enemy planes roared overhead, but I was too occupied to care.

At 7 a.m. the midwife proprietor helped me deliver a boy. My doctor arrived after the excitement was over. He was dressed in his emergency kit as he had been on standby duty all night. I was given a most welcome huge breakfast of bacon, egg and fried bread. It was a time of food rationing, but the home probably received extra rations for the new mothers.

My husband rushed in on 12 hours compassionate leave to see his son. All seemed perfect. But what I did not know was that my young brother of 20 had been lost at sea six weeks earlier. The whole family had kept the news from me until after the baby was born.

Two years later, I was pregnant again and decided to have a home birth. My husband had been injured in the war and was discharged from the army. We were able to buy a sealed sterile package containing everything necessary for the birth. But we were advised to save clean newspapers to protect the bed and floor and mop up blood and the afterbirth.

Our midwife lived in the next hamlet but her able assistant, who did the laundry and took care of new mothers, lived only a few minutes away. She was a strong country woman who always wore the sister's cast-off white coats, beautifully mended and laundered.

The nurse assured me I would have a speedy labour and as time drew near I shouldn't venture on a bus or go far from home. She said her helpmate could cope in an emergency. The poor woman was terrified at the thought of it.

My mother, who came to take care of our little boy, was concerned that my modern bed had no brass knobs. In her day, women pulled on a towel tied around the brass headboard while they were pushing the baby out. She said her midwife told her rude stories because a good belly laugh helped the muscles relax.

I was three weeks late again and during my prolonged labour swore at my poor mother. I finally delivered another boy - even larger.

I thoroughly enjoyed my lying-in. We lived in a bungalow and my neighbours continually popped over to talk to me through the open window. This was the first birth to take place in our circle, so they all chatted to me through the bedroom window. In a few days, I was up and weeded the flowerbeds in my neglected garden. I ended up with a severe cold that probably affected my recovery.

We all shared the available Moses baskets, high chairs, playpens and potties. Maternity dresses were particularly prized as clothing was rationed. Women were reluctant to use their precious coupons if a maternity dress could be borrowed.

Most manufacturing was directed to the war effort so "non-essentials" were scarce. This included potties, and several babies I know used a pudding basin for toilet training. New prams were like wooden boxes on wheels. Mine certainly had no springs.

Winifred
1941

My only daughter was born in 1941, and I had been evacuated from Manchester's air raid dangers to relatives in Macclesfield.

All births were expected to be natural. No alleviation of pain was offered. After about twelve hours of labour the baby was born and afterward there was the unpleasant business of having stitches to repair the tears of the baby's entry into the world.

The post-natal care was good during our fortnight's stay in hospital, with the nurses encouraging and helping mothers to breastfeed. Babies were placed in swinging cots attached to the foot of the bed, and mothers could rock the cradles by swinging their feet. During the night, the babies were moved to the nursery, and much attention was given to allowing mothers to rest. Several days went by before mothers were allowed out of bed, and it would have been dangerous and cruel to be going home after 48 hours as seems to be the practice today. Before discharge, there were lessons on how to bathe and dress the babies.

My identical twin sister Alice had her first baby in 1944. Both our husbands were away on war duty, and Alice came to stay with me before the baby was due. I became concerned when Alice said she hadn't felt the baby move. She was booked into a maternity home in Harpurhey, some two slow bus journeys away from my home in Moston. We had no phones or access to transport and all able-bodied neighbours were away in the forces or employed in wartime factories. So we made our way to the home, and I left Alice there and returned to await news of the birth.

A neighbour whose son worked on important war business had a telephone and agreed to take phone messages. In the mid-afternoon, I answered a call from the maternity home. The news was bleak and harshly conveyed. A baby boy was stillborn and, as next of kin, I was required to visit as soon as possible. Another neighbour took care of my three-year-old daughter while I made the journey by two slow buses. I was greeted in the hall by the nurse. She said I'd been a long time coming and I was to return with a box for the dead baby and then take it to the verger of the nearest church who would find somewhere to bury it.

I gasped. I couldn't do this and asked why the home couldn't attend to it. "We have to look after births not deaths," was the reply, "and disposal of stillborn babies was the responsibility of the family".

So I went to see my twin sister and tried to offer comfort. She reached for the baby basket she had prepared with loving care, and we both wept as we held a little white baby hairbrush and lace-trimmed delicate gowns. I wondered why the staff hadn't tactfully removed them from the locker.

Walking back to the bus stop, I called in at a shop where I had ordered little matinee jackets. The lady serving sensed my distress and put her arms around me. After a long wait, the bus arrived and I took it to my parents' home. They were having a short break in St. Anne's away from father's responsibilities as a Manchester alderman. I telephoned them and incoherently told them the sad news and how I was expected to find a suitable container and arrange to bury my dead nephew. Father said he would take a train home, war trains were very slow, and to wait until he arrived.

I sent a telegram to Alice's husband, Bill. He received it as he was heading out on D-Day landings with the Royal Engineers. He was not to return for 18-months so there was no possibility of leave.

My father telephoned the Co-operative Funeral Service and asked the manager to deal directly with the maternity home and bury the baby with reverence and dignity. He then spoke to Manchester's Medical Officer expressing his horror and amazement that anguished fathers and relatives could be travelling on city trains and buses holding parcels containing stillborn babies. I believe his interventions led to instructions that these sad incidents should be dealt with in a more humane fashion.

We never discussed the traumatic circumstances again, and it was many months before Alice asked me what had happened. I merely told her that her baby had been buried in a quiet corner of the churchyard.

Just a few weeks after this unhappy confinement, Alice was caught up in the wartime regulations that directed all childless women to help with the war effort. Alice spent her days working in the offices of local engineering firms.

After the war, Alice and Bill had a healthy daughter followed by a cherished son. Now we both have grandchildren, and I have great grandchildren. All have been born in hospitals. The one exception is my exceedingly healthy 21-year-old grandson who was delivered by his father in the hills of Japan. His parents were natural birth enthusiasts, and so the wheel turns in the story of having babies.

Doris
1941

When we arrived at the hospital I was examined by a nurse who said the birth would take place within a couple of hours. She told my husband he could ring for information and he left. I was taken through to the delivery room. The labour pains were severe. There was no doctor on duty but a middle-aged retired nurse, whose general behaviour and conversation put fear into me. I had no idea to what extent the body could sustain such pain, and as things progressed I felt quite sure I was going out of my mind.

The following day an angel appeared in the form of a Sister Midwife. She had been on leave but took over and with such competence, care and understanding. My son was born without drugs on the afternoon after admission.

The baby's head was quite elongated and his skin jaundiced, but he recovered before we left the hospital 12 days later. My husband, on seeing me and hearing of my experience, declared never again. But time is a great healer and in 1944 our second son arrived, again with no drugs.

I have always thought that my oldest son's somewhat nervous and withdrawn nature may well be the result of his protracted birth. But he is lovely in all respects and is now an active and loving son, husband and father.

Doreen
1941

Hal and I were married in April 1938. War was looming but it wasn't an established fact until September 1939. Hal joined the R.A.F in October 1939 and went gaily off to be a 'flyer'. However, he was categorized as having low blood pressure, which was fortunate, as within a year most of the young men who joined with him were dead.

His two older brothers married in 1939, and both their wives became pregnant during 1940. By this time I was disturbed that I wasn't pregnant and underwent all sorts of tests and was told everything was normal. I read about taking Raspberry Leaf tablets to ensure pregnancy. One day I was talking to my neighbours when I felt this swimming sensation. I went to the doctor and he asked if my eating habits had changed.

"Tea makes me sick," I replied.

Needless to say, I was pregnant. At the time we were living in a large house that had been converted into two flats. We lived downstairs with the neighbours upstairs. This was in North London as a lot of Hal's early training was at Stanmore. One night the bombs were rather horrific and a very loud explosion sent me rushing upstairs to check on our neighbours. For a long moment I couldn't see Mr. and Mrs. Davis. I thought they had disappeared. But when the dust cleared they were there. A land mine had dropped in a school playing field in the next street. We had some damage but not as much as you would think. However, this close call prompted us to talk about my returning to my parents in Cardiff.

When I arrived in Wales, I was able to book my confinement at a local nursing home. Pre-natal clinics were being established and I travelled some distance every month to the Truby King clinic. There we learned about handling the baby, breast feeding etc. Breast-feeding was then being encouraged whereas, when I was born in 1915, no mother of the middle-class strata would consider feeding her child. Only the very poor and the gypsies would breast feed in those days.

Of course at Truby King we had been told what to expect and how to time our pains etc. Early one morning I called my parents to take me to the nursing home. Instead of rushing off they stopped to make a cup of tea, which horrified me, as I suppose I expected my child to pop out at any moment.

This didn't happen of course and, once I arrived at the nursing home, there was quite a lot of preparation including drinking a full glass of caster oil. Everything proceeded as it should and eventually I was taken to the labour ward. I'm afraid I wasn't as stoic as I intended to be and kept calling for Hal. My son Robin was eventually born and had a pointed head, much to the horror of my dear mother. This was because they used forceps for the actual delivery. Of course the pointed head settled down in a few days, but it certainly gave her a shock.

I spent the next fourteen days in bed. When I did try and get out of bed, I felt dizzy and weak after spending so much time lying down. We were taught at Truby King to feed every four hours so this is what I did. I remember Rob was crying at 1.30 p.m. and there was no way I would feed him until 2 p.m.

Of course, in those war years, we had to be prepared to get our babies and ourselves out of bed when the sirens went. There were quite a few raids on Cardiff but, we were lucky. My father was a warden, and my mum, baby and I would get up and spend a lot of the night under the solid oak table in the dining room.

Because of irregularity after the first birth I had been confirmed as pregnant before I actually was, so we were expecting my daughter to be born in September. So when September came and went I was very disturbed that nothing had happened. Eventually they induced that birth.

The war continued. When Rob was 2½ I went with the children to stay with my aunt in Liverpool. While we were there he was diagnosed at the hospital as having a mastoid – a swelling behind his ear that had to be drained. He was taken from my arms and I was not allowed to see him, except through a screen, until his release from hospital. This was so cruel and I will never forget his screams when they took him away, and his look of unbelief when I picked him up two weeks later. It affected him all his life, as he became a nervous asthmatic.

When the war ended we returned to London. Once more it was not usual to go into hospital in labour unless problems arose. They had begun making tests on the mother's blood and I was told I was RH negative and may have a 'blue baby'. I was confused as I already had two children. They told me it never happens with the first child, but can with subsequent births. Later we discovered Hal was also RH negative so all was well on that score. I attended regular meetings with the midwife and it was unnecessary to call in the doctor. Hal's sister came up from Cornwall to help after the birth. This baby was a very quiet and docile baby and spent a lot of time sleeping, which was good.

In March of 1949 our son Lynden was born. I remember looking out of the window and seeing Hal's footprints in the snow as he went to telephone the doctor and the midwife. There were not many home telephones in those days. This birth took longer as Lynden was a much larger baby. The midwife wanted to bring about the birth without the aid of the doctor. She felt doctors were just an encumbrance. Finally she was forced to call him. I remember as he administered the gas, I heard her say to him, "Don't you find that the use of (whatever the name of the gas) asphyxiates the child?" The doctor was annoyed, especially as he knew I would probably hear, which I confirmed to him later.

By now our council had a system whereby you could register for a home help, and they sent the most kindly lovely lady who did all the housework and the cooking for two weeks after the birth.

Kathleen
1942

My husband took me to the hospital and, after examination, I was taken to a small cubicle and left alone feeling very frightened. I was just 21, and husbands were not allowed to stay in those days.

After three hours the pains got worse. I was taken to the labour ward and my legs were hoisted into supports on either side of me. I was told to push every time I had a pain. "Keep pushing!" they told me over and over again.

Suddenly, a nurse noticed things were not going so well. "Stop pushing" I was told, and she sent for a doctor. I remember the doctor had curlers in her hair and must have been called from bed. She told me she would have to cut me, and I felt the sting of the scalpel.

After a while, a very bloodied baby was shown to me, and they said he was fine. They began stitching me up. I've forgotten how many stitches I had inside and out, but I begged for no more and at last they had finished.

My little son was brought out to me, and they left us alone together for a long time. I was eventually sent to a ward and my son returned to the nursery. The nurse reassured me that I could see him the next morning.

I recovered from the birth but my insides never really healed. I bled almost continually and was cauterised several times in the next 18 months. The doctor told me I should come to hospital for my next delivery.

But three years later, during my next pregnancy, hospital staff looked at me in disbelief when I said I should have a hospital delivery. I was told hospitals were only for first births.

So I fixed up with the local midwife, and she was called at midnight. My husband had to fetch her as she didn't like going out in the dark.

I was torn again but not so badly. My husband fetched the doctor to stitch me up. He was an old man - he'd brought me into the world - and his eyesight wasn't too good.

He had to put on a second pair of spectacles over his regular ones and still had to peer very closely. His nose was almost touching me, but he still couldn't see very well and the midwife had to hold a torch over his shoulder. She kept pulling faces and saying there was no need for all those stitches and that she would have some of them out the next day - she did.

I had no internal examination afterward and just hoped everything was okay. When I had a hysterectomy many years later, the surgeon told me the neck of my womb was badly scarred.

One of the most difficult things about having young babies during the war was the shortage of nappies. You could only buy blankets, sheets and nappies with clothing rations. When I was first pregnant I only had enough coupons for 12 nappies. Thankfully friends gave me muslin liners and second-hand nappies they no longer used.

The laundry was never ending. Babies slept in long flannelette gowns that were tucked in at the bottom. They were always soaked through in the morning.

One of the scariest times of all was when everyone in the village was called to the hall and issued gas masks. I was given a shoebox-sized mask that I was supposed to put the baby in and then pump air in and out so that he could breathe. We never had to use it, but the very thought of it was very frightening.

Olive
1944

My first child Christopher was born in a two-bedroom cottage with a cold-water tap outside and the toilet and washhouse at the bottom of the garden. I had two near miscarriages, which my mother, a part-time Red Cross nurse, helped prevent. She sent for the doctor and put the bottom of my bed up on bricks. I had a couple of weeks in bed both times with the district nurse visiting once a month.

When it came time to deliver my first baby, my mother prepared the bed with newspapers to mop up blood and other dribbles. The nurse came then sent for the doctor who gave me injections to slow the pains down and let me sleep as the baby was very weak.

When my son was born, he didn't breathe. The doctor asked my mother if she had any whisky as he'd seen this work. He poured a few drops into my baby's mouth and he breathed.

He weighed 6 lbs and had epileptic fits from six months to six years. The midwife called in every day, and I was bed-bathed for a week. I was finally allowed to sit out of bed after seven days while my bed was made. The baby was difficult to feed. He just would not suck, and the doctor and nurse said he was a naughty boy. When his weight dropped to 5 lbs, my mother wanted a second opinion. I was 20 years old and too shy to ask any questions.

We took him to the hospital where they kept him in for two months and taught him to feed. I visited the hospital but was not allowed to cuddle him. It was the hospital's way of doing things. This was very upsetting, and my husband kept watch while I picked him up and hugged him.

My second child, Jennifer, was 2½ weeks overdue. The pains started at around 10 p.m. The district nurse was on holiday and my husband had to go to the local hotel to get the relief nurse. She was a missionary nurse and made my parents and husband say prayers around my bed. There was nothing for the pain, and I had to deliver on my back, which was very painful. I was lying on my side for the first birth, and it was much easier. Jennifer was born at around 2 a.m. and again prayers were said around my bed.

The next child was born with little problem. We moved to a council flat converted from an old workhouse. It had all mod cons including electricity and a gas geezer for hot water.

With the fourth I had a lovely district nurse who called every month and, as the pregnancy progressed, she told me to stay in bed for a week. Mum walked a mile each day to take care of us. The birth went well, and Mollie was born at home. No visitors were allowed for the first two or three days after any of my births.

My fifth child, Andrew, was three weeks overdue. We were now living in the country, one mile from a village, as my husband was working on the railway as a fog man. There was just a stationmaster's cottage and our three-bedroom cottage. When it was foggy, my husband had to put detonators on the line to signal the train drivers. I had a small kitchen range and an outside bucket toilet that was emptied once a fortnight by my husband - we had smashing garden vegetables.

Two huge galvanized tanks held rainwater and our drinking water came on a train from the next station five miles away. We used rainwater for laundry and for baths, which we had in front of the fire. We had no electricity, only Tilly lamps which gave good light and warmth.

Our next baby was born with little problem. By this time I had a cold tap in the house and an electric cooker. Annabelle was three weeks overdue but when I finally went into labour, I fed the other kids, sent them to school and tidied the house. I called the nurse from the station and she came with her knitting and a sandwich as it was her day off. I was given the usual enema. My husband arrived in time to help with the birth. The cord was wrapped around Annabelle's neck twice and it had to be cut before she could be born. She also had a caul (a clear piece of membrane) over her face. It had to be removed quickly so she could breathe. Cauls were once much sought after by sailors. They believed if they carried a caul they would never drown.

My last baby is my darling. We are very compatible and I am told that she spoils me.

Margot
1944

My fiancé was called up into the army and, when he came home on embarkation leave in 1940, we got married. In 1942 he was put in charge of a training unit in Huddersfield, so I got a job in Yorkshire and went into lodgings so he could come home at weekends. I thought I was pregnant and the local doctor confirmed this, but then said very casually, "If you had come to me before you conceived I would have said don't bother as you are too small across the pelvis and will have a very difficult labour."

It was not a pleasant thought but, by now, nothing could be done about it. My husband was in military service in Huddersfield and I was working nearby so we could see each other at weekends. For the delivery, my mother booked me into a nursing home near her house in Kent. Unfortunately, before I could get there, a rocket fell on the nursing home and destroyed it.

A kindly aunt in the Lake District took me in. By this time, I had a month to go until my delivery date and had not seen a doctor or had any medical attention. But I had kept well.

When the labour pains started I was taken to the nursing home and put in the general ward. I stayed there for two days and two nights without any attention - they were apparently waiting for my waters to break. By the third day, when I thought I was going to die, the doctor was sent for and I knew no more after that because he pushed a chloroform mask over my face as soon as he saw me.

When I awoke, the doctor said I had a fine baby boy, but I had lost a lot of blood. I took weeks and weeks to recover, and my poor aunt had to look after the baby and me.

Two years later, I decided I would like another baby. But after four months, not seeing a doctor or anyone of course, I miscarried and was very ill in hospital for three weeks. Enough is enough, I decided. I never tried again.

Bonnie
1944

During the war, my husband was a pilot in the Air Force. He was away during my pregnancy, but his brother, a doctor, always looked after me. He took me into his heart and said he didn't want me to go through with the pregnancy. I had liver and gall bladder problems and wasn't strong. My brother-in-law took me to a Harley Street specialist, and they decided I should have a Caesarean Section when the time came.

London was terrible during the war. The air raids were so bad and everything was peculiar. The Harley Street doctor called and said he had to pass me onto another doctor as he was going into the services. He passed me to a gynaecologist, and he arranged for me to have a Caesarean Section two weeks before my due date at a Manchester hospital.

I was sick all the time. I didn't fancy food. All I could eat was carrot soup. As a result, I was discharged from my job with the war office.

I went into labour two weeks before I was due to have a Caesarean. The family doctor called for an ambulance but there was an air raid on. When I did get to the hospital, they had no room for me. I had to go into one of the public wards. It was so busy, women were in the corridors, but there was nowhere else to go. I lay there in a public ward with women shouting and swearing, I'd never heard language like it. I felt so alone. There were bombs falling. I would have loved my mother with me. Every time they came to examine me, I tightened up and was out the other side of the bed.

It was a long slow labour, and my gynaecologist didn't visit for two days. He was furious when he saw me. "Why wasn't I called?" He had a string of students with him, but the baby's head was coming out and he said it was too late to do a Caesarean Section. The baby's head was wedged and the gynaecologist pulled him out with forceps. Every moment was agony. They gave me something to breathe into, but it didn't do any good. I discovered later it wasn't working. And they had my legs spread out on stirrups in front of students. It was quite awful. By the time he arrived I didn't want anything to do with him at all. They put me into a sleep, and I didn't catch a glimpse of him until the next day. He was so ugly. I'll never forget it. In the Caesarean ward all the babies looked like little dolls. The nurse said he will be lovely soon. But I didn't believe her. I was in hospital for three weeks. The whole experience killed my sex life completely. I didn't want anything to do with my husband at all.

Eileen
1944

My husband was in the Navy and didn't see my son until he was six months old because he was sailing to Malta in a convoy.

During the war we lived in Liverpool and used to sleep with my mum and family in the street air raid shelter until daylight. On most nights everyone would go down there straight after work.

My helping hands were my mother and two good sisters. We all lived in terraced houses in the same neighbourhood. We had two bedrooms, a living room, kitchen, and a yard with a toilet. There were no council properties in those days.

My first two children were born at hospital, but the second two were born at home as I didn't want to leave the other two. I had antenatal care at a local school. The midwives who came to the house were very kind and clever. My eldest sister helped me through as she lived in the next street with her five children.

We had a coal fire, no hot water, no bathroom. The children had a bath once a week in front of the fire each Friday night.

The Post-War Years

1946-1950

At the end of the war people were battle weary and tired. There was relief that the threat from Hitler's armies was over, but feelings of joy were tainted with sorrow for the husbands, wives, children and friends who had died. The country lost more than 330,000 people to enemy action at home and overseas.[32]

In addition, Britain had huge financial debts, and there was a tremendous shortage of housing as more than a million homes had been damaged and thousands destroyed during the war.

Shortages continued, and surprisingly, food was more severely rationed after the war than it had been while Hitler was threatening the shores. In 1948, the weekly food ration per adult was 13 ounces of meat, one egg, one ounce of cooking fat and two pints of milk.

Many husbands were weak and ill after spending time in prisoner-of-war camps, and their wives wrote to magazines seeking advice on good nourishment. They were told to give their husbands small but frequent meals with lots of milk, eggs, vegetables, cheese and gravy.[33] In this food starved nation, this was like recommending veal and smoked salmon.

Children were also malnourished. One mother complained that her 3-year-old was anaemic. Give spinach, egg yolk, herring and raisins said the *Home Companion*'s Sister Mary. Another said her 4-year-old was bilious from too much fat. She was told to increase the cereal and jams in his diet. Yet others complained that their children had rotting teeth. Dose them with cod liver oil, said Sister Mary.[34]

Many women sacrificed their own rations to feed children and husbands, and there were frequent banner adverts calling on housewives to take care of their health for the sake of their families. One woman complained on the beauty pages about her thinning hair, saying a hairdresser had refused to give her a perm. Oranges, nuts, milk, prunes, figs, turnip and eggs were recommended.[35]

The launch of the National Health Service in 1948 brought some reprieve. Medical care became free and the improvement in health statistics was almost immediate. Most children were drinking free milk each day and would become taller and heavier as a consequence.[36] In addition, there were fewer babies dying before their first birthday.[37]

Some of the improvement was due to immunization campaigns. Until this time, vaccinations hadn't been a right but a paid-for privilege. During the war more children died of preventable diseases such as diphtheria than were killed by bombs. But successful advertising campaigns in magazines, radio and newspapers brought more children to the nurse's needle.

The NHS also brought standardised care for pregnant women. Most births still took place in the home with the uniformed midwife called out when "the pains" were steady. Hospital births were mainly for those pregnant for the first time or those with difficult medical histories.

Great strides had been made in medicine during the war years. The method of blood transfusions had been improved as army doctors treated soldiers injured in battle. In addition, antibiotics became more available and could be targeted towards specific diseases.

The war had also changed the courting ritual, with many couples throwing caution aside and indulging in sex outside of marriage. As a result, illegitimacy doubled after the war to nine percent of all births.[38]

But there was still a strict moral climate, and unmarried mothers faced cruel choices. A single woman with an 18-month-old baby wrote to a magazine agony aunt that she was soon to be married but not to the infant's father. They were moving into an apartment that didn't allow children, and she was looking for a home for the child where she could pay for his keep. The only option, according to the agony aunt, was adoption or a talk with the clergyman for referral to a suitable carer.[39]

Another pregnant woman wrote to an agony aunt that she was unmarried and no longer liked her boyfriend. *"You will grow to like him in marriage,"* came the reply.

As husbands returned from the services, there was a boom in births. But it ended quickly as couples were confronted with food and housing shortages. Contraception however was limited to the withdrawal method and condoms, which were often in short supply. The only method that put the woman in control of fertility was the cervical cap. But many husbands feared the cap would encourage their wives to have affairs.

Beauty and fashion tugged heavily at women, and there was a real push to get life back to normal – no matter the shortages. As a result, magazines gave beauty advice alongside images of pretty girls decked in off-the-shoulder Hollywood gowns.

"*Why not be as radiant and attractive as ever – just take Bile Beans at Bedtime*".[40]

These unglamorously named supplements would "gently clear the system". Constipation was, according to one magazine editor, at the root of all spots.

Beauty aids were in short supply, but there were plenty of homemade potions that could help. Hair could be kept in place with a setting lotion made of precious sugar and water, and women could rub the hair off their legs with a pumice stone.

Clothes rationing did not end until 1949, but many patient woman worked hard at being fashionable by unpicking old clothes or unravelling old knitted jumpers and making their own creations. *Women's Own* carried a knitting pattern for a full-length two-piece suit that could be made by dedicated knitters. It comprised a long sweater, belt and calf-length skirt.[41]

Going to the cinema became an increasingly popular night out and, by 1946, more than a third of adults said they visited the cinema once a week.

Hollywood became a mirage for women keen to improve their lot in life.

Celebrity lifestyle tips became very popular. In the *Women's Own*, actress Diana Day advised women to always look nice for their husbands by:

Using a pink lipstick even before breakfast.
Doing housework in clothes fit for outdoors.
Occasionally wearing a little girl hairstyle to please her husband.
Wearing a girdle, even at home.
Using regular deodorant.
Having a short rest before your husband is due home from work then redoing make up and hair, changing your dress and putting on perfume.

Such frivolities were all part of a push to prove that the miseries of the war were over. Large white weddings came back into fashion, and magazines gave practical tips for getting the most out of the big day. These included an exotic Prawn Cocktail as a starter. Food rations would allow three prawns for each diner.[42]

Tips on home decoration also crept into the magazine pages, and some of the bold colour schemes could outdo the most flamboyant of designers of *Changing Rooms*. Lilac walls with white paintwork would bring brightness to any room suggested the *Women's Own* in 1947; while a small room might look larger in yellow walls with brown horizontal and vertical stripes.

But large white weddings and new homes to decorate were beyond the means of most young couples. Because of the severe housing shortage, many young couples had to live with parents. As a result, Agony Aunt columns were flooded with letters from young wives saying their mother hated their husband who was no longer the dashing figure he had been during the war.

"I don't know what to do," wrote one young wife. *"I do not like my husband and cannot face the prospect of spending the rest of my life with him."*

The Agony Aunts were unsympathetic and firmly rebuked wives telling them to work harder at keeping their husbands happy. One woman wrote to Mary Grant's Problem Page in *Woman's Own* saying her husband went out most nights drinking and frequently had affairs. She wrote:

"He has a bad temper and has often struck me. I think sincerely we can never be happy together."

Mary Grant came down hard on the young mother.

"Yours is a case where I feel very strongly that I have heard only one side of the story... It is strange that your husband never takes you out now and practices these silly and unimportant little deceptions. I don't want to sound unsympathetic, but are you sure you are not in some way to blame for his attitude?"[43]

Another women, aged 51, wrote that her 54-year-old husband was spending time with a young girl in his office.

"She has an invalid father, and he says he is just helping her out," wrote the worried wife.

Again, Mary Grant discredits the writer's concerns.

There seems no reason to suppose that his interest in this girl is anything more than friendly.[44]"

Despite such autocratic advice, many women did leave their husbands and the post-war years saw divorces increase to ten times their pre-war rate.[45] But separating from a marriage partner wasn't easy, especially when children were involved.

One *Home Companion* reader left her daughter with her husband who was: *"continually nagging and finding fault with me".* She now had her own dressmaking business and felt financially able to care for the child.

But the Agony Aunt was not sympathetic.

"I think you were very much to blame for losing your little girl, even if it was impossible for you to be happy with your husband."[46]

Peggy
1945

My eldest son was born in December 1945. I was fortunate to be living in Blackpool in comfortable rooms. My husband was in the Navy but stationed ashore at the time. I booked in at the hospital maternity annex. We were monitored well before the birth and I had a course of sunray treatment to help with my health.

We also had to take in our own cloths and pads, but all baby things were provided except for going home. I was left alone during labour as they were very busy, but that was not unusual. The final stages were hard, and I had to have stitches, but he was over 9 pounds and I was very small. We had good tuition on the care of the baby and ourselves. I was lucky as I was able to feed all four of my children. The health visitor came often until I was strong enough to go to the clinic.

My second child, a girl, was born in Liverpool in 1947. I had check ups during my pregnancy but not as good as for my son. It was a much busier area, and there was no hope of going to hospital. I was living in furnished rooms with my husband who had now joined the Liverpool City Police. Both houses we lived in during this time had bathrooms and hot water.

I had booked in for my baby's birth at a Salvation Army nursing home. They cared for young girls in need and our fees helped pay for them. The nurses did not leave me alone. In both births I had an injection for pain, but I think this slowed the birth time. I was stitched again. But thankfully, this baby was 2 pounds lighter than the first.

I was able to get an army surplus rubber sheet for her cot but no rubber pants to cover her nappies. I used muslin nappies with terry towelling over the top. For extra protection at night, I wrapped a further nappy around like a skirt. She would also wear a long gown for warmth, so there was lots of washing each day.

When the baby was six weeks old we were told we had to move as the landlady's son was coming home. The welfare officer found us a house in a very old part of Liverpool. It had an outside toilet, but there was no light at all in the yard. The house had gaslight and there was one coal fire and a gas boiler for hot water. Life became very hard. We bought an oil stove and a bungalow bath. A fireguard was a must with a toddler. Shift work for my husband was a nightmare.

Again the baby clinics were very good. The nurses worked extremely hard. We were able to have orange juice and baby foods as we needed them. The hardest job was getting washing dried and aired. A ceiling airer was useful but one had to remember to bank up the fire at night.

After a couple of years, we found another house. It was all-electric and had a back boiler at the fireplace to heat the water. But the toilet was still outside in the yard. Life became a little easier until two years later and I became pregnant again. The children had chicken pox and my husband had a very bad case of influenza. With all the worry and running up and down stairs, I started showing blood. I had to go into hospital where I had a miscarriage and was given a D and C operation. That seemed worse than having a baby. But there were many miscarriages at the time. I suspect a general lowering of our health due to wartime rationing and so much worry.

My husband transferred to the Metropolitan Police in 1952. We moved into a lovely flat overlooking the park in Peckham. It was heaven as it had a beautiful bathroom, a coke-fired boiler for hot water, a fireplace in the main room and wall heaters in all three bedrooms.

Margaret
1946

It was my first pregnancy, the war had just ended and we were undecided in what to do. My husband took a job in the tax office, and we stayed with my parents.

My mother, in her youth, had had a miscarriage. The doctor had refused to come out because we lived in the country and a neighbouring midwife had saved my mother's life. That midwife was still active when I became pregnant and, as far as my mother was concerned, she had angel wings.

She was called out, and I went into heavy labour over three days and nights. I just thought this was normal. My father and husband were going off to work, coming back and the baby still wasn't here.

The midwife had apparently fallen out with my doctor and she didn't want to call him. I still had a great deal of trust in everyone, but she did finally call another doctor as labour was just going on and on.

He came and gave me Chloroform drops on a mask. The baby had to be pulled out quickly because it was in distress. He had bruises on either side of the head and a cut lip from the forceps.

I came round from the anaesthetic with my mother and the midwife saying they didn't know how they were going to get me out of it. Of course, I was torn from ear to ear. I had blood in my nails and hair, and they had to cut my nightdress from me. My mother buried the bloodied sheets and the bandages that were used to stop the bleeding.

I was incontinent for a period and bedridden. I couldn't walk for three weeks and still remember the great exertion of pushing the pram.

He was never a very happy baby.

Later I asked a lot of questions. I was a good swimmer and the theory was that my muscles had become tense with swimming.

They said I shouldn't have another child. But 3 years later – it happened. Contraception was limited. I'd used a gel, and my husband used a sheath. But we must have been careless.

Life equips you for what you have to face. I had no fear and was quite determined. I decided I would have it at home again. My labour started at midnight, and my husband was working in Bristol. I lit the fire and warmed up the house. I didn't wake any of the family, as I didn't want to scare anyone.

I had another son by noon

Looking back, I was very ignorant.

Regarding sex, I'd see two ducks and thought they were having a fight in the trough. We just didn't know about sex. I'm surprised I came out as a virgin. Quite a few girls I knew didn't know the facts of life and got into trouble.

I learned a lot from my husband, but he really didn't know much - his parents were elderly. We'd married quickly on a special license due to the war. He feared he'd have to send me back to my parents just as I was.

Later, we said to ourselves that it is a wonder our marriage survived. I still have the legacy of the births - the wreckage left behind.

Pauline
1946

I was 21 years old and knew nothing. My mother hadn't told me anything about childbirth, and I had no brothers or sisters.

I was booked into a small private maternity home which cost 10 guineas a week. We had to book in for a full two weeks, as the matron would not let anyone in for a shorter stay. She wouldn't even let us put one toe out of bed until 10 days after the birth. The matron had been Queen Mary's nurse when the Duke of Windsor had abdicated and she would sit at the bottom of our beds and talk about her life with the queen.

I was told my baby was due on 4 June, but she didn't appear until three weeks later.

My waters broke on a Monday and the next three days seemed like a living hell. I was offered a gas and air mask. I'd never seen one before and it seemed broken. I eventually threw it on the floor. I was pulling so hard on my ankles that they told me to stop or I would break the bones.

The matron and nurse sat at the end of the bed, nothing seemed to be happening except me going in and out of terrible agony. It must have been at about 5 a.m. on the Wednesday morning that they suddenly said, "It won't be long now. We can see the head." At about this time I had what seems to be called 'an out of body' experience. I was floating on the ceiling. There was no pain whatsoever, and I looked down on myself from a corner of the ceiling. All I could think of was that I had to get back for my husband and baby as they would need me.

Anne, my beautiful daughter, eventually arrived at 5.30 p.m. As she emerged, the matron asked the nurse to quickly pass an injection for the baby. At the same time, she placed a piece of gauze over the baby's mouth and breathed hard into her to get her lungs working. At this point, the cord had not been cut and I didn't know if I had a son or daughter. She was quickly wrapped up and held up for me to see. Her head was the shape of a black and mauve ice cream cone and she had red thumb and finger marks around her forehead. They said the marks would disappear in a week or two and, thankfully, they did.

Matron said that, for my sake, she should have sent for the doctor but he would have used forceps, which would have finished the baby. People say you forget childbirth, but I've never forgotten the experience.

However, two years later I was back at the Bransbury nursing home. This time everything was normal and I was delivered of a beautiful 9 pound baby boy.

After the war my husband came out of the Royal Navy and his work took us to different parts of the world. This meant that our children had to return to the UK for their schooling when they were aged 12. My husband and I missed them a great deal and thought we would start a second family. I was about 37 when I became pregnant and we were thrilled to bits. We were back in England on leave when I started having the most dreadful back pains. I was 5½ months pregnant and was rushed to hospital. All that night there were nurses running in and out of my room. I seemed to be going in and out of consciousness and could feel blood pouring out of me. The nurses kept changing the bed, and I could hear myself saying, "Sorry, I'm so sorry." When I opened my eyes I saw a drip bottle full of blood and a young nurse sitting beside me. I was given seven pints of blood.

Although I was told the baby had been perfect, I know my husband was told which limbs were missing. The doctor told my husband, "This is nature's way of disposing of something which is not perfect."

Earlier in this pregnancy, I had suffered from severe nausea and the company doctor told me, "I have some wonderful tablets that will knock that on the head for you." They did and, at the time, I was grateful. Please remember, this is 1963, we were overseas and had not heard the word "Thalidomide". So when this awful thing happened to us, we were shattered. I wanted to try again, but my husband pointed out that we lived overseas where blood for donation was in short supply.

Nora
1946

I was married in 1937, but because of the war it was nine years before I had my first baby, and by then I was 34.

I was talking in the kitchen one night with a young medical student, a friend of my brother, and he told me, "If you ever get pregnant read *The Revelation of Childbirth* by Grantly Dick Read." A few weeks later I ordered the book and read it from cover to cover.

When the time came, I was excited at the thought of a much-wanted baby. I had booked into a small maternity home in Norwich to be near my parents. My husband was still in the forces.

I went into the nursing home early to escape my mother's cold. The contractions started quietly. But after a 72-hour labour, which was manageable though long, it was finally decided that I must have a forceps delivery. So for me, a general anaesthetic and there was my beautiful, much wanted son.

Two years later, I was pregnant again. We had moved house so another nursing home was booked and another doctor. I went in about 10 p.m. so as not to disturb the household.

The doctor looked in next morning and said he was going to church. I was quite content. Soon after, I rang the bell for the nurse as I felt the baby was coming. I had no time for the delivery room. The nurse bustled around and I had another lovely son. The doctor came back just in time to stitch me up. He had left church early.

For the next baby, I elected to stay at home. I had a lovely midwife. It was her last case. My husband was with me, just chatting. We had begged the nurse to go downstairs and have something to eat. I was on my side, the position I always chose. The head came through. I sent for the nurse and all was well. I had my third son.

The fourth child, I had again at home. I felt I knew all about it by now. The midwife came. She gave me an enema and called the doctor in the middle of the night. It was then I learned she was not qualified to deliver the baby. The doctor came and left - I was not nearly ready.

In the morning, she gave me another enema and called the doctor. He came and after a while the baby was there with the cord around its neck. My daughter was safely delivered. I was 40, my experience only spoiled by the nurse, but I had a lovely daughter.

When I hear of the ways man interferes today, all to be quick. I am not sure that it is better today. My experience was marvellous.

Elsie
1946

My first birth had been normal. We lived in the Church of Scotland Manse just outside Dumfries, and I was under the care of a local doctor who lived two miles away. A private nurse was booked for the birth. She had been highly qualified – second matron in a maternity hospital – but she had come to do some private work to be near her elderly mother in Dumfries.

As the due date drew near, the doctor found it was a breech presentation. He turned the baby himself at my home. He also warned the midwife to stay within a phone call because he was attending the wedding of the Duke of Buccleuch's daughter in London.

The midwife came to stay at the manse at the booked date. The baby was late but eventually I went into labour. It lasted over 24 hours. Apparently, the baby's head was presenting in a bad position.

The midwife called the doctor. He was just setting out on his afternoon visits, and he came straight away. I would not have survived if he had not been able to come quickly. The midwife told me later that the doctor had difficulty in stopping several haemorrhages. I was very weak and remember seeing a long tunnel with a light at the end. I discovered later that this was a near death experience. I breast fed the baby, and he was very healthy. He is now a veterinary surgeon.

I was very fortunate to have the nursing sister care for me. She was very overworked as there were agricultural workers 16 miles further up the glen and she was on-call 24 hours a day. She lived alone in a house and would have had very little time to cook for herself.

After the birth, I had no relatives or friends to help. A cleaning lady came for one shilling an hour. The wife of a minister was very poor as our husband's salary was inadequate. Today, no wife would tolerate what my life was – slavery!

Brenda
1947

My husband was a naval bomb disposal expert and toward the end of my first pregnancy I went to stay with my parents. I tried to get a place in the local nursing home, but they were full and wouldn't even see me. As it turned out, this was fortunate as we had a big freeze. Roads were blocked with snow and I wouldn't have made it to the nursing home anyway.

When I started in labour, the local doctor came and pronounced that the baby would be a long time. He gave me "twilight sleep". But by next morning the midwife arrived and immediately sent for the doctor. He gave me chloroform but I could sense a great panic. It seems that Michael had been ready to arrive hours earlier and the cord had wrapped around his neck as he had twisted and turned in his endeavours.

When I came around I was heartbroken to see this poor baby. All 8¼lbs of Michael were various shades of purple, blue and red. His skin was dry because he was more than two weeks overdue.

After I was tidied up I was given the baby to feed. I wanted to sit up but the midwife, who was retiring at the end of the week, said I had to stay lying down. I lay flat for the rest of that week. The new midwife, a much younger woman, was appalled and had me up on my feet as soon as possible.

The doctor also retired shortly after this. It seems I was given "twilight sleep" because he didn't want to be called out during the night as the weather was bad.

It took four years before I could bring myself to have another baby. This time I went to a hospital, but it was more like a detention centre. I'm sure the sister hated mothers and babies.

I was left alone in the labour room, and because I kept ringing the bell for someone to be with me, they took the bell away. My waters broke at 5:30 p.m. but they said I would not deliver for some time. At 8:25 p.m., I realized I was about to give birth. I shouted for someone to come. Luckily one of the mothers got out of bed and told a nurse I was calling.

After that I had plenty of attention but got a good ticking off from the sister for shouting. Peter weighed 8¾lbs.

The doctor said my next one would be more than 9 lbs. "Oh no, it won't," I told him. "There's not going to be any more." And there weren't.

Michael died of cancer at age 33. I often wondered if his traumatic birth contributed to his illness. St. Thomas's in London said it may have had to do with before or during his birth, but they would not elaborate.

A tailpiece, Michael's granddaughter (our great-granddaughter) was born in 1997. Life goes on.

Iris
1947

You never showed you were pregnant in my day. You covered it well up. My mother-in-law even told me not to go out. She said she would only go for walks at night when no one could see her pregnancy. It wasn't something you flaunted. But the shopkeepers always knew who was pregnant because your ration book was a different colour and you got extra rations. We got extra milk but not much else.

I paid six guineas, around a week's pay, to have my baby at the nursing home. My husband was still in the RAF, so my brother-in-law took me there and dropped me off on the doorstep. It was OBE – oil, bath and enema. The oil was caster oil that you took with dry bread. After the enema did its job, you were put in the labour ward. The midwife would occasionally stop in to see how you were doing, but mostly you were left on your own. It all went okay, although I hadn't known what to expect. No one did the first time. They kept you in for around 10 days. We weren't allowed out of bed for about four days, and you were only given the babies at feeding time. They were all bound up in blankets, they could hardly move.

I went home to my mother-in-law's house. And she told me everything I should be doing. There was no point in disagreeing with her or trying to tell her what the hospital said. I was in her house and I had to follow her instructions. It was so nice when my husband came home and we finally moved into our own house.

With the second birth, the baby came too soon. The midwife didn't make it to the house in time. We knew she wouldn't and my husband had to carry me upstairs to bed. He put me over his shoulder, but the doors were all very low and he managed to hit my head as we passed through. The baby came out so quickly. Then the midwife arrived. She was carrying the gas cylinder into the house, and my husband told her she wouldn't be needing that. She was very cross and said that if anything happened to the baby he could end up in court. But what were we supposed to do?

Joan
1949

I was 23 when our first child was born. I knew absolutely nothing about childbirth and had no idea what was ahead of me. There was no antenatal care, but I saw the district nurse on a few occasions.

We'd recently moved to a small village and our parents were around 100 miles away. Toward the end of my pregnancy, my mother and 14-year-old brother came to visit. On their last evening we sat up very late chatting. When we did eventually go to bed, I couldn't seem to get to sleep. But my husband and I decided it was just indigestion.

After another hour we decided we had better waken mother but we didn't seriously consider I might be in labour. I still had 10 days to go and I wasn't having any real pain. But we started timing the bouts of "indigestion" and discovered they were coming every ten minutes. Like almost everyone else, we didn't have a telephone and my husband had to get dressed and cycle down to the phone box in the village to call the midwife. But she flatly refused to come out. She said she had examined me only a few days before and she was sure I was going to go my full time or even longer. She said we were just first-time parents worrying about nothing and we should go back to sleep.

We were very concerned when my husband returned with this news, as the pains were now coming every five minutes. So off my husband cycled to the phone box again. It was about 4 a.m. by now, and the midwife was far from pleased to have another call. But she condescended to come. When she examined me she was amazed at how far advanced I was and apologized for not coming earlier.

Our son arrived safe and sound at 5.50 a.m. It was nowhere near as painful as I'd expected it to be. My brother was astonished when he woke up in the morning to discover he had become an uncle. He hadn't heard a sound and had slept through all the activities.

The saddest thing for me was that my mother and brother left that very morning. My parents ran a village post office and getting away was always difficult. My father expected them back that day, and a little detail like my giving birth counted for nothing. He was a difficult man and crossing him was not advisable. We all knew and accepted it but hated him for it. If we didn't toe the line, we knew that he took it out on mother and made her suffer and we couldn't allow that.

It did present us with problems though. In those days, a new mum had to stay in bed, and that was difficult as I had no one to help me. My husband wasn't allowed any time off at all. In fact, on the morning of the birth, he cycled down to telephone to explain the situation. He planned to stay home and help. Later that morning however, someone was sent from the office with instructions to get back to work at once.

It seemed so heartless. We had to pay for a lady from the village to pop in a couple of times a day, get me some food, and help with the baby and other chores. It must have been dreadful for my mum to leave her new grandson and me. I know she wanted to help me but sadly it couldn't be.

Compared to the young mums these days with disposable nappies, washing machines, central heating and all mod cons to help them, in 1949 we had nothing like that at all. Washing dirty nappies and all the other things by hand and having to get them dry in bad weather was a real nightmare.

In spite of all that, I think the worst thing was not having a telephone. It was so awful to be alone in the house all day with a new baby and not be able to get in touch with anyone in emergencies. Looking back now, I wonder how we ever survived. But we didn't really feel we were depressed. The sorts of things that are now taken for granted were just not available for ordinary folk in those days.

By the time our daughter was on the way we had moved to Weymouth. We lived a few miles outside town and, this time, I did get a little bit of antenatal care. It meant travelling five miles to the nearest hospital, and it was very difficult struggling on the bus with a lively toddler and a pushchair.

But my antenatal care did not start out well. After having a blood test, I was told by a very officious nurse that I had no right to be having this baby. I was completely bewildered and didn't know what she was talking about. She said I should know I had an unusual blood group and having a second baby could be risky. I told her I had never had a blood test before but I don't think she believed me.

She shouted that I ought to get rid of the baby and look after the one I already had. I flatly refused and was told that if I went ahead with the pregnancy the baby would die or be a "blue baby" and need a complete blood transfusion. This was something I had never heard about, and it was dreadful to be made to feel at fault.

Naturally I went home upset and worried. My husband and I discussed it at length and, although we now knew the risks of my being rhesus negative, we decided to go ahead with the pregnancy.

Except for worry, the whole pregnancy was trouble free. Three weeks before my due date, I was busy doing laundry. After hanging it out in the garden I went into the house to make lunch. But suddenly I was hit with a dreadful pain, which literally made me collapse in a heap on the floor. I couldn't get up until it eased and I had to explain to Christopher that mummy had a tummy ache. I tried not to worry him, but within minutes it happened again. I knew then that without any gentle build up, I was in the last stages of labour.

I did feel panicked and was concerned about our two-year-old. I had no way of getting help. Next door was too far away and again we had no telephone. This is when a miracle happened. There was a tap on the kitchen door and when I crawled over to open it, there was my mother and brother. They had decided to come for the day. It was absolutely wonderful to see them. What I would have done if they hadn't turned up right then, I just can't imagine. It's a terrifying thought even after all these years.

Mother could hardly believe I was in the last stages of labour, but it soon became obvious. She sent my brother to call an ambulance from the village phone and she kept an eye on little Christopher and me. We waited thirty minutes for the ambulance while the pains came faster and faster. The ambulance crew was from another county and they lost their way trying to find our road. As if that wasn't enough, they looked at me in horror and said they had never had a maternity case before.

It was a harrowing journey with the pains coming thick and fast. The ambulance man didn't know what to do other than give me his hand, which I'm sure I bit very hard on occasions. It seemed to take ages to reach the hospital. I tried not to give birth in the ambulance but I felt that once I arrived at the hospital the baby would come with the next pain.

I was in a pretty bad way as the ambulance men carried me in on a stretcher. As they took me up a flight of stairs, we met a dragon of a sister. She was furious and told me I had to walk. She didn't allow her maternity cases to be carried in.

By then I had had enough. I told her that if she wanted the baby born on the stairs then it was okay by me, but it was going to happen soon. Reluctantly she told them to take me to the labour ward and before the ambulance men left, my daughter had arrived.

My mother had sent a message to my husband at the office and, although his colleagues told him it was pointless to phone the hospital yet, he got through to the labour ward in time to hear his daughter's first cry.

From the first pain in the kitchen to our daughter's first cry was just 1½ hours. So much had happened in that time that I was left trembling afterward. The dragon sister did have the courtesy to apologize to me afterward.

Now that it was all over, the greatest relief was knowing that, in spite of all the doom and gloom from the antenatal clinic, our daughter was absolutely perfect. We were so thankful. But I was concerned about what was happening to my son. I had to wait until my husband visited that evening to learn that my mother had left Christopher with a neighbour so she and my brother could return to dad as planned.

Yet again dad and the family business came before a new baby. It was such a coincidence that my mother had been with me on both occasions and purely by chance. I felt bad that she hadn't been able to stay long enough to visit her new granddaughter. I suppose I knew it would happen that way, but that doesn't make it any easier. We had to arrange for my mother-in-law to come out and take care of Christopher while I was in hospital. The new baby weighed only 5lbs 6oz so we had to stay in hospital for a couple of weeks before she was allowed home. She made wonderful progress, and we were just so thankful that all went well. I'm glad I didn't listen to that awful nurse in the antenatal clinic or we shouldn't have had our little daughter at all.

Ivy
1949

I had a boy of 3 and a daughter of 10 months when my twins were born. I didn't know it was to be a twin birth until my waters broke. I'd been out shopping and rushed home. When the midwife told me, I tried to put the best face on it, but my mother was shocked.

The twins were 4lbs and 4¼lbs. No one took them away. They shared a crib and, although I'd breast fed my first two children, I knew I couldn't feed them and bought the new powdered baby milk. No one told me to get food for premature babies or that I should be feeding them low-fat milk. The baby food made their little bottoms raw. They were screaming all the time and I had to leave them without nappies. The health visitor thought I wasn't looking after them properly. An older woman told me to put them on cows' milk and Robertson's patent barley. It worked.

The twins thrived. But they got so much attention and no one looked at my bonnie baby of 10 months. I was lucky that I had my mother for help. We lived with her until three months after the twins were born.

My husband was still in military service when my first son was born in 1946. I wasn't too sure what would happen but I'd read stuff in books and women's magazines. When labour started, I remember sitting in bed thinking that I could cope with this. The later stage took me by surprise. I really felt I was being torn in two. The midwife sent for the doctor. He told me I wasn't very popular because he'd been having dinner. He then he plonked Chloroform on my face, and I woke up while I was being stitched.

For this extra treatment I had to pay the doctor a larger fee.

But having the babies was not as difficult as the coping afterwards. I never did master the art of rubbing things with a scrubbing board. My hands were raw. They never healed because there was always something needing scrubbed.

And married life was difficult. Neither my husband nor I had a lot of knowledge about birth control and it was a chain reaction - you didn't want him to come near you because you were afraid you would have another baby.

My husband was very possessive and jealous, and I was young and naive. I went to a birth control clinic and was fitted with a cap. But my husband used to say I'd been using it while he wasn't home. I threw it in the fire. I was so young and so stupid. There was no help. You just accepted everything. I had to rely on his withdrawal. But we are all products of our time and we were not unusual.

There was a certain amount of prejudice when you had a large family. People thought you were a bit feckless and not terribly capable. But eventually the health visitors left you alone because they realized you were capable. The best help came from my mother.

There was no harm in the long run. I'm healthy, although having six children doesn't do a lot for your figure

Kay
1949

My waters ruptured at 10 p.m. and, shortly afterward, the contractions began and the midwife was notified. She arrived the next morning and called the doctor later that evening. He sent me to the Central Middlesex Hospital where I was placed on a trolley in a corridor. The next morning, I was transferred to a small ward and, a few hours later, transferred to the labour ward and left alone again. At 3.30 p.m., almost two days after my labour had started, I managed to attract a passing nurse and made her understand that I wanted someone to do something.

I was anaesthetized and, on regaining consciousness, was informed that I'd had a daughter, 7lbs 4ozs, at 4 p.m. by forceps delivery.

I was placed in a ward and had a 10 minute visit from my husband. Visiting was then Wednesday evenings, 7-7.30p.m. and weekends between 2-4p.m.

During the next two days I saw neither my baby nor any visitors. On the third day my husband visited me in the afternoon. He had viewed the baby through a glass panel in the nursery and he assured me that she was well.

Finally, four days after giving birth, I saw and held my baby – so much for bonding!

From then on she was delivered to me every four hours for feeding.

My next baby was born in Hammersmith Hospital. The sister said she intended this to be a normal birth, and she delivered my son and let me have a quick look before he was taken off to be cleaned up. Once again, babies were in the nursery and handed out every four hours for feeding.

I went into labour early in my next pregnancy. The midwife and doctor arrived at the house in the evening, and a son, 6lbs 8ozs, was delivered at 12.03 a.m., and then – surprise – a second son, 4lbs 8ozs, at 12.10 a.m. There were no scans then! The bigger baby had concealed the smaller one. But the bigger baby was blue and taken to hospital. He died after two days. The smaller baby thrived, but it was hard work with lots of hot water bottles and three-hourly feeding. It was a real family event.

With my fourth baby, everything was normal. I finally got it right!

The Recovery Years

The 1950s

As the country moved out of the post-war doldrums, a greater sense of optimism grew. Restrictions eased and shops began to stock more foods. But there was still little in abundance. The rationing of milk, flour, eggs and soap ended in 1950, but restrictions on the sale of meat went on until 1954. In addition, the post-war housing shortage had led to huge increases in rents charged by private landlords. To keep prices affordable, the government stamped out rent rises. As a result, landlords had no incentive to improve their properties and housing conditions deteriorated.

In 1951, most homes had electricity[47] but one-third of British houses had no bath. In some homes, children shared not only a room but also a bed. In London and Glasgow many families lived in one-room flats and had to share a lavatory with seven other families.[48] In most cases fuel for heating and for hot water was dependent on coal, which was stored outside and lugged upstairs.

The government began a serious campaign to improve housing conditions, and there was a push to build new towns in the countryside where families could have gardens and fresh air. It was hoped that the general health of the population would improve in more spacious conditions.

Young married couples with children were given priority for the new homes, and they happily moved out of the cramped back bedrooms of their parents' houses. Such was the thrill of the new home that most were keen to put a personal stamp on the dwelling. Great emphasis was put on style and all things sleek and new. Furniture was streamlined. Kitchens had fitted cupboards rather than freestanding shelves. Heavy porcelain sinks were replaced with sleek stainless steel. And new domestic appliances made household chores faster and easier. The two most popular machines were also the cheapest – the electric iron and the vacuum cleaner. Refrigerators and telephones were still too expensive for the average housewife.

Even washing machines were not a priority. In 1958, only 29 percent of families owned this most valued household appliance[49]. Dishwashers were also a distant dream, even for those who could afford them. An advertisement for a dishwasher in 1958 touted a machine that ran on cold water and "washes, rinses and dries in only 4 minutes".[50] The advertisements for this machine didn't run for long, which infers that the machine wasn't entirely effective.

In magazines, great emphasis was put on cooking and dining. There were still suggestions on improving basic ingredients, such as making tripe tastier by adding sage.[51] But cookery writers gave advice on using new ingredients such as garlic, pasta and rice.

Surprisingly, after all that post-war hunger for good food, fashion favoured the slim, and dieting became a pre-occupation for many women.

Knitting and home sewing were still popular among women who wanted to wear new fashions and not pay shop prices. Ready-made clothing was expensive, and one shop owner insisted that women trying on her clothes should put their head into a paper bag to prevent their lipstick and makeup from soiling her stock. She said she was tired of shoppers asking for discounts on marked clothing.[52]

Until now, young women had worn the same fashions as their mothers. But the 1950s saw the beginning of a separate culture for young people. Music, fashion, hair and even speech patterns all began to mark a new generation. For the first time, clothes were marketed specifically at teenagers.

In addition, attitudes toward children changed. Less emphasis was put on obedience and discipline, and many parents took pleasure in indulging their offspring. They wanted them to have a better life than they had experienced, and they were more likely to play with their children, take them on trips and generally listen rather than give instruction. Because of improved diet and better health care through the NHS, young people had never been healthier. In the 1950s, British children grew taller and heavier than they'd ever been before.[53]

In magazines, the rigid rules from spinster nurses were replaced by the kinder gentler philosophy of Dr. Benjamin Spock. His book, the *Common Sense Book of Baby and Child Care*, told parents to trust their instincts. He encouraged parents to hug their children without fear of spoiling them, and not to worry about feeding and toilet training regimes.

This was also a time when the medical profession admitted to making mistakes. Pregnant women had been receiving X-rays to help with pre-natal diagnosis since the 1920s, but in 1956 doctors linked ante-natal X-rays with the development of childhood cancers.

This caused some questioning and doubt of the medical profession. In maternity care, a challenge came from the newly-formed National Childbirth Trust, who wanted greater information to be given to mothers-to-be so they could make decisions on their labour and they wanted to have fathers allowed into labour rooms. They argued that the medical establishment were wrong in their strictly managed care of women in labour. The group proclaimed childbirth as natural and advocated pain control through knowledge and breathing.

But all the changes left many young women confused about listening to the soft new approach that stressed instinct and emotion, and the old routines that came from their mothers, which emphasised giving babies strict four-hour feeds and to let a child cry rather than risk spoiling him.

The growth of new housing estates also pulled large family networks apart. Newly-married couples were sent to the suburbs, and young mothers, once dependent on their own mothers for advice on child rearing, were now more susceptible to the messages they received from the nurse or health visitor.

Magazines ran letters from young mothers caught between the advice of a health visitor who said children needed more orange juice and their mother who warned that syrup of figs was the answer.

The agony aunts frequently echoed the advice of the health professionals. In the end it was the mother's advice that was often ignored.

The magazine agony aunts also took a kinder and gentler approach to family problems. One woman wrote to Mary Grant at the *Woman's Own* that her husband drank too much and had lost his business. "Leave him," advised Mary Grant of the *Woman's Own*, and get a Maintenance Order. "He may go further downhill and not be able to provide support." Ms. Grant recommended the National Marriage Guidance Council for help.[54]

One husband wrote to Mary Grant that he and his wife were both working to save for their own home, but his wife wanted him to help with housework at weekends. "Surely it is her place to see to the running of the home."

Thankfully, Mary Grant called him "unreasonable".[55]

But some of the male film stars needed to move with the times. Actor Dirk Bogard wrote an article in a 1950s *Woman's Own* outlining the kind of woman he would like to marry.

She should:

Not smoke in public
Not wear high heels with slacks
Wear only a little skilful make up
Never draw attention to herself with loud laughter, conversation or clothes
Never order from a menu when he is with her
Never laugh at him in front of his friends, only laugh with him

Never welcome him home in the evening with a smutty face, the smell of cooking in her hair, or whining about the trials of the day.
Want children but don't be hysterical about them.[56]

The cinema and magazines delivered the idea that marriage should have romance and companionship. This was very different to life before the war when there had been little dating, and couples met and married if they appeared suitable to one another. [57]

Even with all the changes, sex, was still not discussed. A young woman wrote to a *Women's Own*:

"My boyfriend and I are very much in love, and I'm afraid we are inclined to carry our love-making too far. I worry very much that one day we shall do something very wrong."

The agony aunt's reply was that they should take up a hobby such as cooking or carpentry.[58]

Ann
1950

I became pregnant soon after our marriage. Sadly, I miscarried our first baby. We got over our loss and big disappointment, and I became pregnant again almost immediately. It seemed a long wait as I was just over one pregnancy and into the next. Everything was okay, I was in good health and quite optimistic. But toward the end I got toxaemia and had to spend the last week in one of London's teaching hospitals.

Time certainly dragged on, and in those days only husbands were allowed to visit the maternity ward. Finally, on Sunday March 12, I started labour and felt sure that it would all be over by afternoon visiting time when my husband would arrive. But I was still there watching the clock by 2.30 p.m. and no baby. I lost interest in time as I knew my husband would be back again at 6 p.m. The baby was pushing her way into the world when someone shouted that the head had gone back. Suddenly a mask was plonked onto my face, a pen pushed into my hand and I was told, "Sign here!"

I don't know what time I came around, but I was still in the delivery ward. I asked about the baby, and two nurses dashed out the door and never answered me. Then I overheard someone say that when my husband arrived he was to go first to the office.

They wheeled me out to the ward, and my husband came along. I could tell he wasn't full of the joys of spring.

He said, "We have a little girl. I saw her through the nursery window. She's a little bit like you and a bit like me. But she's not very well. The doctor will come to see you in the morning so don't worry and try and get some sleep."

But I knew full well that he was very worried. He looked so sad. There were four other mothers in the ward and it was obvious from the silent nodding and remarks that they guessed all was not right. I didn't sleep much and I cried a lot. The next morning the doctor came and told me that the baby was not very well and that a specialist was coming to see her. He said she could not live for more than a week, and there was nothing that could be done for her. I was sick, sore and very sad.

My husband visited each evening and reported that he looked through the nursery window and she still looked the same. I asked the nurses and Sister what was wrong with my daughter, and I got the same reply each time. "When you get up, you can go to the nursery and feed her." I never got to do this. She was brought to my bedside only once, and she was so wrapped up that I just got a glimpse of her face.

Ten days after her birth we were to be discharged. I was sent to the doctor's office and told that my baby had spina bifida and might survive three months. The doctor said only one in ten such babies survive birth, and that I would be able to have more children. The sister wrapped my daughter up in her shawl and we were sent home. I had no idea of the problem until we got home. Her lower back was very deformed and her right leg was totally paralysed.

For the first week I cried every time I bathed and changed her. Elizabeth was a beautiful child with pleading blue eyes and flaxen hair. I soon learnt to cope and told myself that where there is life, there's hope. As my husband left for work in the mornings, he would say, "Look after her but don't get too attached. We may not have her for long." On his return, he would take the stairs three at a time. He was so anxious for her.

The hospital had given me a formula of cow's milk plus limewater. Our landlady was very kind and tried to be helpful. She could see we weren't getting much medical advice and notified our G.P. He saw Elizabeth and said it was a pity she had survived. I had different ideas though. The sister from the clinic called and seemed surprised we had not heard from the hospital. When it came time for my postnatal appointment I took Elizabeth along and asked the doctor what her chances were. He thought she was a very strong baby but made no other comment. They changed her feed to Benger's food as it was pre-digested. She took so little that she had to be fed three-hourly. She gained weight steadily and seemed to be thriving. But the sister said she would never sit up. When Elizabeth sat up, they told me she would never walk. There's nothing better than trying to cheer someone up, is there?

When Elizabeth was eight-months old, I put her on the floor to crawl, and she crawled until she was 4½ years old. She got through the usual childhood ailments and thrived. She was very bright and intelligent and when she was 20 months old, we had another daughter whom she adored. We named her Patricia, and Elizabeth gave her a pet name,

Patty Pud, because she said she was round like a pudding.

When Elizabeth was two years old, we went to Great Ormond Street Hospital. After a lengthy session with three consultants, plus their retinue, we were told not to bring her again as there was nothing that could be done.

I was very upset, but my husband said, “She’s no worse than when we brought her this morning.” It never occurred to us to put pressure on the medical profession, as we felt she had already suffered enough.

In 1952, when Elizabeth was a little over two and Patricia a baby, we moved to a house in Stevenage new town. What a joy it was to have our own front and back door and lots of space. This was the early days of the town and most families consisted of young parents and small children.

Elizabeth longed to join in the games so I put her toys in the hall and left the doors open. The children soon came in to play with her, and gradually she ended up outside with the gang. Building work was still going on so there was sand and muck galore and they wallowed in it. My spare time was spent between the sewing machine and the washing, which meant standing at the sink. I had to make clothes for Elizabeth as store-bought garments didn’t fit. But I cadged old skirts etc off the neighbours to keep up with Elizabeth’s demand for trousers, and I bought little boots for her. We had a shoemaker call weekly and put extra toecaps on them. The NHS was in its infancy then, and we were never offered any extra help.

When Elizabeth was four, we decided to look for a suitable school. It wasn't a case of putting her away. We wanted her to be educated as she was very bright and intelligent. She could read, spell and do simple sums. We approached the county council and the assistant medical officer paid us some visits. He couldn't find any school that was suitable, especially as we wanted her to have a Catholic education. Then I remembered a photo I had seen on the front page of the *Saturday Evening News* seven years earlier. It showed a nun playing snowballs with a group of handicapped children. That photo, by some magic, had registered in my mind and it now played a fundamental part in Elizabeth's life. I blurted out the name of the hospital mentioned in the article. The assistant medical officer was a very patient man. He looked rather dubiously and, while shaking his head, wrote down the information I gave him. In a couple of weeks, to our complete delight, we had a letter requesting us to present Elizabeth at St. Vincent's. They were good enough to accept her as a pupil.

Naturally, there were a few tears. But she soon settled in. Over time, she learned to use crutches, and by the time she was 6, she was well away and confident. For seven years, we visited every Sunday and at Christmas and Easter. We brought her home for holidays. She passed her 11-plus and moved back home so she could attend St. Francis College in Letchworth, travelling on the bus with the able-bodied children.

When she was 16, she said she'd had enough of school and wanted a job. She started as a clerical officer at the Land Registry in Stevenage. Eventually she became an executive officer. She had many friends and bought her first car when she was 20. She used hand controls and travelled far and wide. I remember the day she took her driving test. I was as confident as she was and went out with the scissors to remove her L-plates.

During her working life, Elizabeth had kidney failure several times. But she recovered quickly and discharged herself as soon as she could. All her friends were able-bodied and a number of them were nurses. She enjoyed swimming, joined the Dolphin Club for disabled swimmers and arranged discos for the group. One of her friends married a Canadian she met at a folk festival they'd attended, and Elizabeth visited her in Canada. She toured around Ireland and knew her way around France. She visited China with friends just after it opened its doors to the west in 1982 and had plans for Russia.

I could go on and on about Elizabeth's independence and achievements. She became ill in November 1983. She died age 33. It was very sudden. We all thought she would rally as she had done before.

One of her outstanding features was that she never left the table without saying "Thank you, Mam."

June 1953

When I was 18, I knew nothing about childbirth, although I soon found out about sex. At check-ups, you were prodded and sent home, prodded and sent home. No one told you anything.

I went into labour and at the hospital I was shaved, given a very hot bath, an enema and then left on my own. The next morning, the baby's head came out. I waited 24 hours to be stitched and was left in stirrups for two hours - decorators and everyone went walking past.

I didn't see the baby for 24 hours. Finally, she was given to me for 10 minutes then taken away again. The baby's nappy was wet but they told me it wasn't time for it to be changed.

When I was pregnant again I wanted a home birth. I'm a normal working class mum and didn't rate very highly so I was told to deliver at the hospital.

My waters broke when I was about 8½ months. I waited a few hours before calling the midwife and when she came at dinnertime she said my waters had not broken. "You've pissed yourself," she said.

Four days later, I started haemorrhaging and became very ill. I was put in the hospital. While I was getting a blood transfusion the ward sister came to see me and told me my baby was dead. She said I'd still have to go through birth, and that I should be okay as I had a child to go home to.

During birth I was losing consciousness, they were slapping me to keep me awake. In my dreams my grandmother came to me and said she would take care of the baby for me. I wasn't aware that my grandmother had died the night before.

I do remember I saw the doctor throw the baby in the basin. I asked to see it but they wouldn't let me. The doctor told me not to be a silly girl. He said the baby goes in the stoke house. They put me in a room facing the stoke house and, with every puff of smoke, I was thinking that was my baby.

Every July 12, I think of him. I do relive that pain.

After three days, they brought me a baby whose mother had died and asked me to feed it. I really bonded with that baby. But then I was sent home and got milk fever.

During the third pregnancy I had taken three Thalidomide tablets. I stopped as soon as the deformities scare came out but I worried about it.

After birth, the babies were swaddled and you couldn't unwrap them to look at their arms and legs. I did - I wanted to look to look and see that everything was okay. The nurse and doctor said he was healthy but there was always some doubt in my mind. I looked at him, checked everything and the nurse was cross. But I got riled and said it was my baby.

The nurse had brought him out complete with a bottle. I said the baby didn't need it, and she said cheekily "What are you going to feed it with?"

"Nature's glands!" I told her.

We were not allowed to move in bed. The babies were fed at set times and not ten minutes before. They were wheeled out on a trolley and we were terrified they would fall off. Half the time you were given the wrong baby, but the nurses got upset when you said anything.

The midwives were mostly unmarried. They suffered from malignant virginity. They had no feeling. They were just like nuns. A woman who'd had Siamese twins was put into a normal ward with mothers and babies. You could have been giving birth to a dog.

Margaret
1953

I had my first child at home with no problems but, my mother told me I should go to the hospital for her next one. So I went to the hospital and told them I was in labour. They said I wasn't ready, I said I was. I was put on a trolley but before we reached the labour ward the baby was born. The nurse said, "You were right."

I'm fast. They didn't believe me. They were wheeling me when he came out. But, the way they cut his cord, it was too close and his naval ruptured. He needed surgery at 18 months and now he doesn't have a belly button. All he has is a row of stitches.

I was kept in hospital for a week. My baby developed a spot - like a boil - and I was put in isolation with my baby. I was left to feed my baby, wash my baby. But no one said what was wrong. The day I was going home, the nurse said it was because my milk was too rich.

"You're a bloody good mother," the nurse said. Other women had to stick to hospital times but, because we were in isolation, I was just left to get on with it myself. But I'd been worried. No one had said anything to me.

With a home birth, the midwives were damned good. We got bathed in Dettol down below - you felt clean. You were in bed for a week. The other kids were around and just came into the bedroom to see the new baby.

I never liked to be fiddled about with. My doctor examined me and that was it. I just sailed through. I smoked and I drank and had sex up till the last; and all my babies were big - most over eight pounds.

I wouldn't be mauled about with. I've got my own ideas and my own views. No heal test, no vaccinations, none of that. They wanted to give my babies the nappy test to make sure the baby was okay in the brain, I think they were just guinea pigs.

I had my last child in 1971 and I refused the needle in the heel (blood test for cystic fibrosis) - a thing like that would give babies brain problems, - and never saw them (the health workers) again for four years.

Elsie
1950, 52, 53

My first son was born at Queen Charlotte's Hospital in London. We lived with my mother in London at the time and the doctor I was attending sent me there. It was a wonderful hospital. But it was a long labour, more than two days. I was in a lot of pain, but all we had was gas and air.

I was kept in bed for a week, we were only allowed up to sit in a chair. During the second week they let you out of bed for a while longer and showed you how to bath the baby and care for him. It was lovely because being a new mum; you didn't know what to do.

We lived with my mother until the second baby came along in 1952, then we were given a council house in Hillingdon. It was lovely. It had a hot water boiler, and we bought oil-filled radiators. In my mother's house it was all coal fires and we had to boil water. The nappies were all towelling. You had to soak them, boil them and then hang them out when we could. In bad weather, clothes just hung out in front of the fire. I did a washing every day. I even ironed my nappies to make them softer.

Our third baby was born in 1953 and, when he was six weeks old, our oldest son Phillip died of polio. It happened very quickly. The doctor thought he had the flu. But when Phillip got worse, I called the doctor back. He said he was sorry, but they would have to take him to hospital. They did a lumbar puncture and said it was polio. They moved him to St. John's Hospital and put him in an iron lung, but he died within a week. 1953 was a bad year for polio. We didn't have vaccinations at that time and we were lucky the other children didn't catch it.

Our fourth and fifth children were born at home. It was a good birth and the midwife brought all the equipment with her. You put it away in the bedroom and didn't touch it because it was sterile. After the birth, the midwife would come in twice a day, bathe the baby and give you a wash down.

We weren't very well off, but luckily my husband had a little car for work and he used to go and bring my mum around to help. Although, with the last two babies, the council gave us a home help for two weeks. She was really wonderful and would come in at breakfast and stay until dinner. It was a great help as there was so much to do. You had to walk to get the shopping as you couldn't get on a bus with a big pram.

Margaret
1954, 58, 62

My doctor handpicked his patients for his nursing home. They were the more educated women. The rest went to the hospital. The first labour was long – 24 hours. The nurses always gave you a shave and an enema. I'd taken relaxation classes but they were no help at that time. But the nurse must have given me something because I remember feeling vague. I lost a few hours, and I remember looking out the window watching two birds copulating thinking, "You don't know what you're up to."

It was a teaching hospital and there were a lot of trainee midwives around to witness the births. As soon as I was in full labour, I was put in the labour room with my legs in stirrups. I remember lying on the bed with the doctor framed between my legs. He was talking with another doctor about going out that night.

All the mothers had wonderful care. We were kept in hospital for 10 days, in bed for most of that time. It was the four Bs – bottles, babies, breasts and bowels. Every morning, after the night staff went off duty, we were given sterile silver bedpans for our douche. I think it was with Dettol. Every afternoon we had to lie on our stomachs for two hours. I think it was for rest but also to help flatten our stomachs.

I breast fed the baby for a few months and would also express milk into a bottle for the premature babies in the nursery. I would leave a full bottle of milk outside my house every night, and a little man would come along and leave me an empty bottle. I did this for about three months, and then I found I was getting tired.

The second baby was born in a private nursing home attached to a hospital. We'd moved to another town by then, and I wrote to the doctor asking if he would take me on his panel. He was a very old-fashioned gentleman, and I think he appreciated this approach. His colleague did all the maternity cases. I was utterly relaxed with the second. All the relaxation classes I did with the first pregnancy kicked in. I wanted to use the toilet, not the bedpan, and the nurse very reluctantly let me. The baby was born shortly afterward.

The third pregnancy occurred when Thalidomide was considered a miracle cure for morning sickness. I always felt sick in the first three months. The doctor asked me if I'd like something to relieve this. I refused saying the sickness would go away in time. I'm so grateful I did. I had this baby at home. I used to go to keep-fit classes with the midwife. I had an appointment with the doctor about three days before the baby was due, but the midwife said I should stay at home. My two previous babies had been born early, so maybe she didn't want to take any chances. She examined me and said I was dilating. She called by later with my "birthing package" which consisted of tarred paper to put under the bottom sheet, some disinfectant and other things. She told me to call her when labour started. She also gave me something to help me sleep and said I would only waken with a very strong labour pain.

She was right. I woke in the early hours. My husband stayed in the sitting room, and the baby was born just an hour later. I think women are idiots for letting men in on this secret refuge. Apart from anything else I was too busy to have a man fussing over me.

Babies were put outside in every kind of weather – even in winter. The only exception was in foggy weather. In the days of coal fires and factory chimneys, the fogs were quite frequent. I would put a wrapped hot water bottle in the bottom of the pram. In summer, when they were older, my children could go outside in the playpen. It had a wooden floor, and I could see them from the kitchen window.

Babies wore two nappies, one of terry towelling and another as a muslin liner. Both needed washing, and laundry always took time. I would soak my nappies in Milton. They were always snow white. For my last baby I used disposable nappy liners. They were a new and extravagant purchase, but saved nappies from becoming too heavily soiled.

We lived in a new bungalow. It had a tiled kitchen and bathroom. Everything was new. The kitchen was beautifully fitted, and the house even had central heating. Something I had never had before. But we really had to save for it. I stopped work when I was pregnant with my first, and I did a little job sewing clothes at home for small dolls. The company paid a pittance, but it was pin-money for me. I took some of the clothes I made to my keep-fit class and showed them to friends who bought them for their own daughters' dolls. After that I had a good little business. I sewed a lot. I also did my own baking. I've never been one for sleeping a lot. I'd get up at 6.30 a.m. My husband left for work shortly afterward. I'd put the washing on, feed the children then walk the older one to school. It was a busy time, but I don't regret any of it. I would always take time for myself in the afternoon, relax in a lovely warm scented bath and make myself attractive for when my husband came home.

Vera
1957

My labour began during the night with pains every few minutes. In the morning, the midwife stopped at the house, checked me out and said, yes, I had started. She came by several more times that day, but she couldn't stay. She was too busy. By the next morning I was in agony. She stopped by again and gave me an injection for pain. It really helped and I was able to get up and have some tea. But it wore off after a few hours, and it was back to all the pain.

The midwife kept stopping off at the house, but I still wasn't ready so she would leave to go off on her rounds again. I was alone in the room. My husband would come into the bedroom occasionally to see if he could do anything, but there was nothing he could do. He would just come in and out. In the evening, the midwife came back and said I should leave the lights on if I needed her during the night and she would see them when she passed by in the car and would know to stop.

So I left the lights on. I was in agony. She came by and called the doctor. He tried everything. He even sat on my stomach to help push the baby out. In the meantime, I wasn't really with it. The pain was dreadful. The midwife was taking my blood pressure. And through everything, I heard her say, "We'll lose them."

The doctor sent for an ambulance and they got me straight into surgery. It was too late for a

Caesarean Section, the baby was too far through, and I heard them say "forceps". I just wanted them to put me out of this agony.

The matron kept telling me to put my knees down. I had them up at my shoulders. But I couldn't bring them down. The anaesthetist let me squeeze his hand, but the matron told me to stop it. Thankfully, they gave me a full anaesthetic. The oblivion was wonderful. But when I awoke it was still agony. Steven was a 9½lb baby.

I really should have had a Caesarean Section. It took me five days before I could pass urine, and my piles and everything were just hanging down. For two years, I couldn't walk properly because I felt everything was falling out. I knew it wasn't going to fall out, they told me that, but it felt like it. I would walk with my legs pulled together to keep everything in.

Two years later they gave me a ring to keep my womb in place. I still go back to the doctor every year to get a new one fitted.

The whole experience was horrible. Sometimes, at night, it all comes back to me like a nightmare. There was none of that exhilaration you hear about when people have a baby and their husband stands holding it and smiling. He was a lovely baby, but the experience was all so awful. It's why we never had another child.

Marian
1958

My husband and I lived in two rooms with my overbearing and distant mother-in-law. Parents did not seem to be so warm and loving as those of the present day. They did not offer help and support and did not assist in any way – they did not seem to enjoy their children. It was more a life of correcting offspring and this continued until adulthood.

I was a State Registered Nurse but did not work after I married. It was not the accepted thing for wives to work or have a career. After I became pregnant, I visited the GP once in his surgery and attended the hospital a few times. The professionals did not explain anything about the pregnancy or the delivery. I had a fear that I would not do what was expected of me.

My husband was on the night shift when I went into labour. My mother-in-law telephoned the hospital and put me, and my bag, into a taxi. She then went back to bed. I had a son by normal delivery with the dawn. He weighed 8 pounds 13 ounces, and I needed stitches.

I was kept in a hospital bed for seven days – until the stitches were removed. I can still remember the agony of trying to get on and off the toilet when I was finally allowed on my feet. My husband visited me for a short time on his way to work. This was a concession as it was not regular visiting hours. My mother-in-law visited on the Sunday afternoon, three days after the birth.

The baby was kept in the nursery at all times except for feeding. Mothers did not bathe or change their infants. They just sat bored in bed. I had started breast-feeding but gave up as my nipples became very sore.

Within a few weeks of the birth, we moved into a semi-detached house. We thought it was heaven, but it was primitive by modern standards. It had no carpets, washer or dryer, and only one coal fire and a two-bar electric fire to heat the whole house. The town and nearest shops were two miles away and we had no car, so it was walking with the coach-built pram.

Within months, I was pregnant again. My son was not yet walking, but no family members volunteered assistance and my husband was expected to work normally. In the end, my mother-in-law said she would come to stay "when the time came".

This was to be a home-birth as routine cases did not go into hospital after the first birth. I bought a carry-cot, a pram seat and a small electric fire for the bedroom. I collected the bed sheets, draw sheets etc. for the home delivery and life went on as normal until the expected date.

My waters broke as I was calling my husband for his night shift. He ate the meal I had prepared while I put our son to bed. We didn't have a telephone, so he stopped at his mother's house to call the midwife, and I promised to send him a message on whether the baby was a John or a Margaret.

The midwife and my mother-in-law arrived together at 6:30 p.m. The midwife said the birth was imminent and there was no time for an enema. She offered me whiffs of gas and air, but I did not like the loss of control it gave me.

A baby boy was born at 6:45 p.m., and the midwife told me to start work again as there was another baby. I really thought she was joking. I wanted to rest. She convinced me I still had a job to do and the second baby, a girl, was born by breech delivery ten minutes later. My mother-in-law was sent to find more bedding and clothing for the second arrival.

I shivered for hours with shock. The doctor made a lightening visit, and a message was sent to the factory to tell my husband it was a John and a Margaret.

I did not sleep that night. I was worried about how we would find the money to keep them and I was so frightened they might die. I decided not to try and feed the babies myself. Instead, I fed them on the then popular tinned Carnation evaporated milk, which was later delivered in the caseload by my brother-in-law.

When my husband came home in the morning, the midwife told him to bury the placentas in the garden. Relatives came around to look at the babies. My parents came for a few hours at the weekend. I can remember feeling so desperately tired and worried about how I would cope.

I was not confined to bed for this delivery. For two weeks, the babies were kept in the bedroom with the electric fire. I went shopping on the fifth day and my mother-in-law returned home on the sixth.

The midwife visited a couple of times and told me to attend the clinic. I did go once, but my life was so absorbed with feeding, washing and sewing that I did not have the time. By the time I had done one feeding and toileting round, the first was crying for his turn. There was no time to think. I just reacted to the needs at that particular time. The government paid parents a weekly stipend for each child, and I used the money to pay a woman to clean the bedrooms as I couldn't leave the children downstairs while I did this chore.

I cannot remember being unhappy, although I can remember imploring my sister-in-law to baby-sit one afternoon when the twins were around six months old. I felt desperate to have a few hours with my husband and no children.

Margaret
1958, 62

My husband was in the navy, so when labour started on the Friday my mother took me to the nursing home. My waters broke and nothing else happened. So the nursing home sent me to the hospital, but nobody told me what was going on. The labour ward was in two parts and I could hear a girl screaming from the other side. I wasn't screaming. I had no breath left to scream. But I was terrified.

The midwives kept going to-and-fro. Some of them were in training, and they had to see so many births. So they left me alone. I could hear this girl screaming, and I didn't know what was going on or what was going to happen to me. That was the worst. Not being told anything, not even being spoken to.

When I eventually had my daughter three days later I had one foot in the stirrup and one around someone's neck. By that time I didn't care. She was coming face up, that's why it took so long. But no one ever told me. It wasn't until I got home, my doctor read it in the notes and explained it to me. I was badly torn. He said he couldn't have coped with the birth.

The nurses weren't very friendly. Because my husband wasn't there they thought I was a single mother, and they would just pass over the baby and tell me to feed her. That was it. She used to cry a lot and I'm sure it was because we were both so upset by everything that had happened. I even had to insist that they let my mother see her. They just thought I was a single mother and not worth anything.

Going home was scary as it was just my daughter and me. I was terrified, but I managed. My mother used to come and do the washing. But the toilet was halfway up the garden and it wasn't even a flush, you had to sluice it with a bucket of water.

There was no hot water in the house; you had to boil water on the stove. Thankfully, we bought a house soon afterward. It had an indoor bathroom and a hot water boiler. I even had a washing machine with an electric mangle. Drying everything in rainy weather was awful. You just had to hang things on a clotheshorse in front of the gas cooker and at night put up a washing line across the kitchen. Later, I got a drier. It was a metal cabinet the size of a fridge. It had rails to hang things and you plugged it in and it dried clothes overnight.

When I got pregnant again, I made the midwife promise that she wouldn't send me to the hospital. She was lovely. She came in when labour started and stayed there. My husband was in South Africa at the time, so I'd sent my daughter to my mother's house. It was a much easier birth. I was able to walk around when I wanted to. At the hospital I hadn't been allowed to do anything. Afterward, I paid a neighbour to do the housework and shopping.

Shirley
1959

I gave birth to my first child in July 1959. I worked until I was six months pregnant. I was quite healthy and didn't have any problems. I attended a pre-natal course at the health centre to learn all about birth. The class included a film of a birth with all the sound effects, which frightened us all to death.

To get booked into a nursing home in 1959 you had to have a medical condition or a social reason for giving birth there, you did not have a choice. We were saving for a house at that time and lived with my parents. It was quite a strain. My mother's health wasn't that good, and my husband couldn't take time off work to look after me so my doctor recommended me to a nursing home.

The last time I went to the doctor, he said the baby's head was in the engaged position and birth could be at any time. I was doing the ironing a few days later when I started getting pains in my bottom. I didn't take any notice because from what I had learned you got pains in the front. Anyway, after a while I decided to ring the nursing home and ask their advice. The telephone box was at the top of the road. They told me to come in and they would examine me - and to bring my case. My dear Dad had an old car and we all went there, my husband, mother, father and the dog. It was midnight with a full moon - a lovely clear night.

My husband rang the bell. I was invited in. The nurse told us to say goodbye, and the door was closed in his face. I will never forget the feelings I had of being totally alone and very frightened about what was to happen. They had obviously decided to keep me for the night and see what would happen. I was given a bath, an enema and a sleeping draught, which I promptly vomited all over the labour ward floor. They were very busy and I was immediately unpopular.

I still only had pains in the back passage. Another girl was brought in, and the only place they had for me was in a corridor. It was pitch dark, and I was told to get some sleep.

The pains in the back kept coming and I held onto the iron bedstead. I must have made a noise because one of the nurses came and told me to be quiet or I would keep others awake.

It was so hot - it was stifling. I just kept pulling on the old bedstead. I forgot all the training I received in pre-natal classes.

Eventually, a couple of midwives came with a torch and said, "Look at this!"

One of them gave me an injection of pethidine and they wheeled me further down the corridor. I gave birth to my daughter at 4.55 a.m. with one leg on the window sill and the other around the neck of a midwife with the hospital stoker, who lived down the road from me, walking in and out of the nearby stoke house.

It was such a relief to give birth and know that my daughter was sound. But it was so sad that my husband could only ring up at the appointed time of 9 a.m. to be told he had a daughter.

The visiting was very strict - only two people allowed between 2 and 3 p.m. and 7 and 8 p.m. If someone else popped in unexpectantly, that was too bad - you had your quota.

We had to stay in bed for six days and only allowed to go to the toilet in a wheelchair. I had stitches and the heat from the rubber mattress used to draw me. When they bathed our bottoms it was bliss.

My baby would not suck. No matter how they tried to make her she just wouldn't, so feed times were a nightmare.

Breast was best and that was that. She defeated us all in the end and had to go on the bottle. I was bound up from stomach to armpits with tight crepe bandages to stop my milk from coming through.

When it was finally time to go home, my husband and father came to collect us. As my father leaned over to pick up the suitcase, the matron came thundering down and told him to get out of the home. We left with our tails between our legs but with utter relief.

The Years of Change

The 1960s

The war years were a distant memory by the 1960s. People were keen to look forward, not back, and glossy advertising in magazines and on television led many dreams and aspirations. There'd been a huge boost in the number of homes and this was joined by an increase in manufacturing as factories had switched from armaments to consumer items. The boom in production led to a fall in prices making the cost of items such as refrigerators, washing machines, small cars etc. more affordable than ever before.

The growth of television occurred in the 1950s so that, by the early sixties, 75 percent of homes were receiving programmes such as *I Love Lucy* and *Ready, Steady, Go*, the forerunner to *Top of the Pops*.[59]

Advertising in magazines escalated pushing must-have items such as ready-prepared meals and veneered furniture.

Style and home décor mattered more than ever before. Emphasis was on all things new. Shapes were sleek, and colours bold.

Washing machines moved out of the outhouse and were now tightly tucked under kitchen countertops. On laundry day most had to be wheeled out of their corners and hooked up to the kitchen taps.

Ownership of washing machines grew to 64 percent during the 1960s.[60] In the late 1950s, only 8 percent of homes had refrigerators, but this number leapt to 69 percent by 1971. Luxury goods such as electric blankets, automatic tea-makers and Pyrex non-stick dishes, were also on offer to tempt those who wanted that little bit extra in life.

The top choice in flooring was the fitted carpet. Previously, most homes had been floored with linoleum which was topped with a square or rectangle of carpet in the 'front room'. But now carpets came in a dizzy array of patterns and colours to stretch from wall to wall. Adverts for carpets were often set against geometric wallpaper and patterned contact paper, a new concept in shelving. The whole mix created some epileptic designs in home décor.

Fashion was also zany with women still knitting and sewing, but not so much out of necessity; instead it was to put their own stamp on trendy designs. Magazines moved away from conservative advice that women should spend their clothing budget on one or two classic outfits.

"You'll be bored stiff with them before you can afford something else," one fashion guru told her readers in 1963. *"Cheap clothes will give you just as much wear and just as much pleasure for half or one third of the price."*[61]

The old standby dishes such as Toad in the Hole and Shepherd's Pie were far from chic. New foods crept onto the kitchen table with recipes in magazines for chicken curry, taramasalata, and crepe suzette. Articles advised which wines should accompany meals, for no hostess could risk getting such a thing wrong. Foods were now new and scientific. Advertisements touted artificial sweeteners, non-fattening chocolates and specially-made baby foods. Up until now baby food was simply home cooked and ground through a mincer or, if you could afford it, a special wind-through sieve designed for infant foods.

Mothercare opened its doors in the mid-sixties selling everything for the modern mother. Baby alarms, baby baths, even disposable nappies were now on the market.

Magazine editors also moved with the times and finally acknowledged that all was not well in the suburbs. In 1968, *Housewife* magazine ran an article on women and alcoholism focusing on the story of a young wife who turned to drink while lonely. Her husband travelled a great deal, and she drank to feel warm and happy. Her husband complained that the house was a mess and his wife looked "old". The journalist followed the wife through mental health counselling and ended with the couple reconciled.[62]

The magazine also printed a story advising single mothers on how to be good parents. Illegitimacy rates increased during the 1960s to eight percent of all births[63], but until now, few journal articles even acknowledged that a child might be born without a married mother and father.

Agony aunts, however, were still naive to readers' problems. One woman wrote to Mary Grant that she had a good marriage but was feeling a strong physical attraction to her husband's best friend. She said he frequently visited the house when her husband was out. *"Get your health checked"* was the response, so that she would know that the physical side of her marriage was okay. Then she should find a hobby so that her days were not so empty.[64]

Advice on careers for women was still limited. In 1965 a girl wrote to an agony aunt that her parents wanted her to be a secretary but she wanted something more exciting. She was told that secretarial work would be exciting if she worked for a business tycoon or a newspaper editor.[65] Another article advising young women on careers suggested work such as a telephonist, sales girl, nurse or, for the really high achiever, an air stewardess.[66]

The world did widen out for many people in the 1960s. Domestic air travel doubled between 1961 and 1971.[67] Package tours to Spain, France and Italy drew many to foreign climes and spurred interest in foreign foods and habits.

And it wasn't just holidays that lured people away. During 1960s, more than 100,000 Britons per year migrated to places like Australia, Canada, New Zealand and the United States.[68] Some were urged to action by an assisted package scheme where governments, such as that in Australia, subsidised travel and helped new arrivals with jobs and benefits. Many were roused to travel by package tours where they'd enjoyed a sunnier climate.

Birth rates fell in the 1960s as contraception improved and became more available. But despite all that is written on promiscuity in the 1960s, a 1969 study showed that 63 percent of women and 26 percent of men were virgins on their wedding night. Among married couples only 19 percent of couples used the contraceptive pill, 29 percent used condoms while 37 percent used nothing at all.[69]

The sixties did bring greater independence for women. In 1964, the Married Woman's Property Act allowed women to keep half the money they saved from their housekeeping allowance. Three years later, the Matrimonial Homes Act gave women the right to half the house in cases of divorce.

Health care, especially for pregnant women, was dominated by a drug scare. Thalidomide, a sedative heavily promoted in the 1950s for morning sickness, was abruptly taken off the shelves in 1962 after a link was made between the drug and the birth of severely deformed infants. From that time on, all health professionals took a more cautious approach to prescribing medicines in early pregnancy.

Esmeralda
1961

During my first pregnancy, the baby was breech. I was given a general anaesthetic and the doctors tried to turn the baby so the head was coming first. But the whole procedure made me bleed.

For 14 days I waited in hospital for labour to start. The labour ward was close by, and I could hear the women groaning and moaning. Pregnant women were kept alongside mothers who had delivered their babies. The older and more experienced women talked about difficult births, and I was terrified. The sister told me a little knowledge is a dangerous thing. During this time my husband was only allowed to visit me for one hour a day, and my parents could only come for one afternoon a week.

When you are a young girl with your first baby, you don't like to ask questions. I heard a story of a young girl losing her baby after it was put on a hot plate by mistake.

Finally, my labour started. One of the new mothers held my hand through the early pains. I was told not to push until my waters broke. I did my breathing exercises to stop pushing. Finally, the waters broke. They were all a dirty green colour. Everyone seemed to be panicking, and the registrar was brought in at midnight. The staff rushed around and I was put on another drip because my contractions had stopped. They started again but when my daughter born she didn't breath properly for three minutes. She now has epilepsy, it started at age 13, and I wonder if the birth was responsible.

Breech babies were given special care so I wasn't allowed to have her in the ward.

I had the next two babies at home. Stephen, my third, weighed 11¼lbs. The midwife was a young girl who was new on the district, and it was the biggest baby she had ever seen. She called the doctor as she feared the birth had ruptured my bowel. I was rushed to hospital, but luckily I was okay.

Patricia
1962

I went to see a doctor when I realized I was pregnant. By then I was four months. The doctor examined me and said the baby was breech. He sent me to hospital where they gave me a full anaesthetic and tried to turn the baby, but it wasn't successful. So they told me I'd just have to give labour a try, but that I'd probably have a Caesarean Section. Then they sent me home. I didn't hear from anyone after that. Neither the doctor nor the hospital sent for me.

I was working as a bus conductor on a double-decker bus. It was quite hard work and, in my spare time, I made my baby's layette. I'd always wanted a baby and I wanted everything to be special. My husband wasn't very interested though. He had his own life.

The day before I went into labour, I contacted the hospital because things felt strange. The baby wasn't very active – he used to stretch a lot and push his head under my ribs – so I felt there was something wrong. They told me to come along when I was in labour. The next day the pains started. The nurse examined me and asked if I'd had a bath recently. I told her no but I'd had a strip down wash. We didn't have a bath in our house, not many people did in those days. She said I'd do. Anyway, I was in labour for eight or nine hours. They gave me gas and air, but it just made me vomit. They finally said, the baby was stuck and there was a doctor on his way to give me a caesarean section. I felt awful. I was so sick and in such pain. A sister stayed with me while they got me ready for theatre and, as she took me down in the lift, I asked her if this was it – would they put me out so this would all stop? She'd let me hold her hand, and her fingers were all bruised the next day.

I was so ill afterward. The stitches were so big and deep, and there was so much pain you would be pouring with sweat. But they only gave painkillers every 12 hours. It left me feeling terribly uncared for.

My husband was not involved at all. He didn't visit until the second day. Even then he wasn't interested. When we got home from the hospital all he wanted was a loan from the maternity grant I'd got from the government. I needed things from the shop, but he wouldn't take us in the car, and I didn't have a pram. So I wrapped the baby in clothes and then in a tablecloth and carried him inside my coat. My husband beeped the horn at us when he drove past in the street.

It was all a struggle. But I'd handmade Stephen's layette because I'd wanted him so much. I didn't have a lot of breast milk, and they'd supplemented his feed in the hospital with powdered milk. When we came home, he cried a lot. I finally called the midwife and she said he was starving so we put him on Ostermilk.

We had a coal fire in the house, but it was so cold that we used to live and sleep in one room. But when I gave Stephen his first bath, he turned blue, and I realised the room was still too cold. I had no money for things such as a clothes horse or shelves for the baby's clothes, but I bought a bit of wood and made my own. We kept everything near the fire for warmth and air.

I had three months maternity leave. By the time I was due back at work my husband had disappeared. I went back on the buses and we had a good nursery run by the council. But shifts were difficult. At first I had a friend take care of him, but that didn't work out. Then I brought in a live-in nanny, but that took all my money and I learned you couldn't trust them. So I got a job as a matron in a boarding school, and I was able to have Stephen with me. It wasn't well paid – £20 a month – but it was free board, although I had to find other jobs during the school holidays.

Looking back it was one long struggle. But I was always very close to him. I'd wanted him so much. I did cry a lot, but there weren't a lot of times when I felt couldn't cope.

Anonymous
1968

My son was born in 1968. Among the strict health checks was always the dreaded internal. After my first internal the doctor decided to fit a metal ring in place as my womb was slightly tilted. I had not had a miscarriage before or lost any blood. I have never heard of someone else having this.

But I had other problems. Just walking into a hospital for a check up and my blood pressure would rise. So a date was set for me to enter hospital for induction. Labour started while my husband was visiting and, after he left, I was given an enema and a bath. I was then left on my own thinking labour would come at any time.

I was left on my own for hours and felt very frightened. Finally, at 1a.m., I had a forceps delivery of a baby boy. They tried to phone my husband, but no one answered. I was given a cup of tea and expected to sleep.

I spent ten days in hospital. So much pressure was put on weighing the baby after each feed. I can remember being tearful like everyone else when your baby didn't gain weight. Babies were kept in the nursery except during visiting hours, which were only in the evenings.

When we went home, the health visitor visited every few days until she thought you were fine. After nine months I became depressed but coped and went on to get pregnant a few months later.

I didn't need a ring with this pregnancy because after the birth my womb was tilted the right way. I lost a little blood and had high blood pressure so I was induced. It was a very quick birth in the afternoon and my husband sat outside till our daughter was safely delivered. I again suffered from depression and received electrical treatment.

My son was a difficult child and couldn't read at the right age. They blamed it on a difficult birth – there was no name then like dyslexia.

Today, I envy mums not being left on their own during labour.

Sandy
1962

I'd like you to think of one of those "kitchen sink" style early 1960's drama films - grey, gritty and harsh – because that's how my world felt being pregnant and unmarried in 1961. At the time I lived in London and worked in Croydon as a sales assistant in a large store. I loved working hard at my job, and even in those days Croydon had become a large, bustling town. It was a wonderful challenge to make my displays attractive and vibrant enough to catch customers who might otherwise have taken their custom to one of the many other stores in Croydon. My boyfriend was older than me, and he made me feel very secure. There seemed little to worry about until that fateful week when my period failed to arrive.

My work colleagues were the first to discover my secret because I lost weight and spent a lot of time in the ladies cloakroom throwing up. These days, I suppose, a fifteen-year-old girl might be suspected of suffering from bulimia, but that condition was unheard of then. My girlfriends commiserated and cried with me. Older married colleagues approached me in the corridor and whispered cryptic messages about "gin and hot baths" and some mysterious potion from the chemists named Widow Welch's Pills.

It was frightening, the comforting days of my periods had gone, and my boyfriend soon followed suit. Now there was no other option. It was time to tell Mum.

Perhaps my story would have turned out quite differently if we had been middle class and comfortably off. After she had recovered from the shock, Mum muttered things about "little operations", and "if only we had the money". I was not much more than a child, and didn't really understand what she was talking about. It must be borne in mind that abortion was strictly illegal in 1961.

Looking back, it was a time when England was just coming out of the dreary post war decade of rationing, utility furniture, and shortages. A time of new kinds of music; the first beginnings of "youth culture"; people enjoying new television programmes; trying out more exotic foods and dressing in a far sexier way than ever before.

Everyone perceived the age as progressive and contemporary. And, yes, to an extent it was – but feminism had yet to arrive – within the working classes at any rate. The dream of most young girls was to float down the aisle, pure and pristine in virginal white. Sexual mores had become, if anything, stricter than during the unsettled war years, and the birth control pill was still in the laboratories and not generally in use. It was summer 1961, and to a young, pregnant teenager, it might just as well have been 1861.

Life settled down into a routine of work and home, although I seem to remember coming in from work and spending a lot of time in my room, the atmosphere was strained to say the least. Also I still felt quite tired both physically and emotionally.

After a few weeks, the very thing that I had earlier so longed for occurred. I started to bleed. It happened at work, and now that the pregnancy was confirmed and accepted, it was scary. Did I really want to lose the baby I was carrying? I was rushed into hospital and ordered to have complete bed rest. I spent many weeks just lying there. I was sixteen years old by now, but still far too young to consider asking a lofty consultant what kind of injections and tablets I was being given. Also, they had me frightfully drugged up most of the time, and I seemed to have spent a great deal of the hospital stay feeling half asleep. I dread to think what they were administering to me. I have half suspected that some Thalidomide was given; this is because of research I carried out on the internet after both my daughter and I developed cancer in later life. It was widely used for anti-nausea and sedative purposes, but was withdrawn later that year, I believe. Thankfully, Coral was born without any defect, so if it had been administered she remained unscathed.

Once they'd managed to check the awful sickness and nausea, my appetite returned. I particularly remember how delicious the food was - beautifully cooked chicken in a light sauce was a favourite, such a luxury then. I wondered why the woman in the next bed wasn't having such delectable fare, and asked the nurse. She laughingly replied, "You've been on a special building-up diet that's why, it's back to normal next week though". Sure enough, the food the following week was stodgy and what one might expect in hospital. Thank goodness I was discharged shortly after.

By the third trimester, I was home and feeling better. Regular antenatal checks at the clinic confirmed that everything was as it should be. The clinic staff, however, would not do very well in these days of politically correct speech. Those stiff and starchy nurses relished the fact that I was a "Miss" rather than a "Mrs" - the title of "Ms" hadn't been invented. My name was called out extra loudly and with great emphasis on the "Miss". All the married mothers, happily expectant as they were, would glance at me as I walked past them toward the doctor's examining room and then gaze smugly at their wedding rings. I was young and resilient, but can you imagine such humiliation being tolerated now? It all seems very silly and petty and part of another world.

Christmas 1961 was almost with us. My job was hard work but fun, however the rush hour travelling was beginning to exacerbate the fatigue of late pregnancy. The fashionable four-inch high-heeled shoes we all wore then didn't help much either!

Six weeks before my due date, it was time to enter the "Home for Unmarried Mothers". As with most experiences in life, there were elements of the mother and baby home that were quite tolerable, even pleasant, but other aspects of my three-month stay there were somewhat harsh. I loved the large, rambling old house with the adjacent little chapel, and, during that spring, the huge garden was a myriad of beautiful shades of green and yellow. Elderly houses, however, need plenty of TLC, and who better to perform this service than "the girls". From dawn until dusk we worked at hard and heavy tasks. Spending the morning on one's hands and knees scrubbing the kitchen floor the day before labour started was considered beneficial, and we were told that it would help 'open' our wombs, therefore making for an easier birth.

I met many different girls at the Home, some were as young as thirteen years of age, and they were very frightened at the thought of childbirth - understandably so. Another, older girl, was a pretty red haired vivacious girl of nineteen, and I can remember feeling quite in awe of her. I loved to hear her talk about the two passions in her life - her man and her job. Her man was of the married variety so that seemed a bit of a non-runner to me, but her job sounded fascinating. It was with something called computers, and involved a primitive form of what is now known as Data Entry and involved punching holes in cards which could then be inputted to deal with payroll and other clerical tasks. At the age of sixteen I'd never heard of anything like it before - little did I know that I was destined to become a computer programmer and have a lifelong love affair with these fascinating electronic animals!

It was a February night when the first tummy pains occurred. I was in a long dormitory full of peacefully sleeping girls, and the little clock ticking endlessly by my bedside. But my tummy pains just would not go away, I imagined they were caused by indigestion, and longed for dawn to arrive to enable me to get out of bed without disturbing anyone too much. This was how I spent the entire first stage of labour without even knowing what was happening. It was rather a lonely experience. At last the hands of the clock told me it was six a.m., and I was able to get up quietly and have a wash. It was here in the washroom that my waters burst and I went straight into second stage labour. Everyone else still asleep, I padded across the dorm and downstairs to the resident nurse. The Home wasn't set up as a Maternity Unit, and the procedure was for us to give birth in the local hospital, coming back after a ten day stay on the maternity ward.

I think the nurse was rather alarmed at the thought of my baby arriving in the middle of breakfast. Just as with any other institution, the lynchpin of the Home was routine, and everything ran smoothly because procedures were adhered to. It was very strict and, at the slightest suspicion of contractions, one was ferried off to the hospital. I can remember her shouting down the phone for an ambulance, saying, "Please hurry, she is bearing down already".

This woman was normally serene and tranquil. She practiced yoga and was a vegetarian. We respected and liked her, but thought her somewhat eccentric and quirky. Her alternative style of living was a little ahead of its time. The fact that this, normally calm, woman seemed agitated rather bewildered me. I was even more puzzled by the resounding "No, Sandra, you must not!" when I asked if I could just pop along to the toilet. My ignorance of what was really happening to me was appalling; I had no idea that my body wanted to push the baby out there and then!

The ambulance arrived, and the regular waves of pain were becoming quite intense, almost doubling me up and taking my breath away each time. The hospital where my baby was born was not far, around three miles away, but at that hour of the day the rush hour was beginning. In between the powerful contractions I could hear the ambulance bell ringing away merrily (no sirens were fitted on emergency vehicles at that time). We were weaving around buses and cars, and seemed to be driving really fast. The nurse turned to me smiling, and patted my hand, "I bet you haven't travelled in an ambulance with the bell ringing before!" Well, at that time I couldn't have cared less even if I'd been aboard Santa's tinkling sleigh complete with reindeer pulling me along. I only wanted to get to the hospital and have my baby. This child would certainly galvanize the on-coming day shift nurses into action as she quickly and efficiently burst upon the world.

The two young pupil midwives who attended me were a caring, but not particularly calming, influence. There were times when they seemed so nervous that I wondered who exactly was having this baby! I was told afterwards that I had been an excellent model lesson for them in how to deal with a straightforward but extremely quick birth. There hadn't even been time to get me into a hospital gown before it was all over and done with. One little procedure from the standard midwifery practice of the time always makes me want to smile. As they were trying to get me into a position to give birth to the baby, I saw one of them produce a tape measure and proceed to measure my girth. At this point, Sister appeared as if from nowhere, and said crossly, "For goodness sake, Nurse, what on earth are you doing?" Stammering, the poor trainee said she was trying to measure my uterus. Sister was not at all impressed with this and told her in no uncertain terms that the birth of the baby was imminent, and she should forget all about such niceties!

Afterward the birth came the exhilaration of knowing all the pain had been worthwhile; the comfort of a clean nightie, and a wash and brush up; or maybe, that glorious cup of tea. You know, it really is the best tasting cuppa in all the world. For me, it was the feeling of achievement, I'd been through something special, and yet, it was the most natural process of all.

But over the next six weeks at the Home, I saw much heartbreak and many tears. Now living in the mothers' wing with my little daughter, I witnessed first hand the agony of girls having to give their babies for adoption. A small handful didn't seem to mind too much, but most broke their hearts as the dreadful day approached when the social worker would call to take their baby son or daughter away forever. I vowed that I would never see my beautiful baby be given away to a stranger. My story has a happy ending because my parents fell in love with my little daughter too, and I was allowed to keep her and bring her home.

My parents have long since passed on, but I shall always be grateful to them for the fact that I was able to keep Coral. There is something tremendously gratifying about seeing her happily chatting with her younger sister, the two of them exchanging their modern day tales of pregnancy and child rearing as my grandchildren play together.

There's only one pretty child in the world, and every mother has it

(old proverb)

About the author:

Yvonne Barlow was a midwife in Scotland, Zambia and the United Arab Emirates before leaving the profession and studying journalism in Texas. She worked for The Dallas Morning News and took up freelance journalism after returning to live in Britain. Her work appeared in English language newspapers around the world. But she never forgot her midwifery experience. A chance comment by her Scottish granny made her curious about childbirth for previous generations of women.

Index

Endnotes

---

[1] Euripides: Medea
[2] The Workers Birth Control Group, Westminster, 1928
[3] Fleming, Stuart. "Musings on Midwifery", *Archeology*, Jan/Feb 1988: 69
[4] Aveling, J.H., *English Midwives*, 1872, London, AMS Press, 1977
[5] Hughes, Muriel Joy, *Women Healers in Medieval Life and Literature*, New York, Books for Libraries Press, 1968
[6] Leavitt, Judith Walzer, Science Enters The Birthing Room, *Journal of American History*, September 1983, pp 285
[7] Holmes, Oliver Wendall. "The Contagiousness of Puerperal Fever". *Classics of Medicine and Surgery*. 1843.
[8] Smith, F.B., *The People's Health: 1830-1910*, Holmes and Meier Publishers Inc. 1979
[9] *Maternal Mortality: Report of Meeting Held at Central Hall, Westminster*, The Maternal Mortality Committee, 1928
[10] *Home Companion*, 10 July 1943
[11] *Home Companion*, 3 July 1943
[12] *Woman and Home*, September 1943
[13] *Home Companion*, 20 November, 1943
[14] *Ladies Mirror*, 5 February 1941
[15] *Home Companion*, 3 July, 1943
[16] *Home Companion*, 20 November 1943
[17] *Home Companion*, 20 November 1943
[18] *Women's Own*, 19 October 1940
[19] *Home Chat*, 26 April 1941
[20] *The Home Companion*, 25 December 1943
[21] *Home Companion*, 17 July 1943
[22] *Women and Home*, October 1943
[23] *The Home Companion*, 20 November 1943
[24] *The Home Companion*, 10 January 1942
[25] *Home Chat*, 4 January 1941
[26] *The Home Companion*, 11 July 1942
[27] *The Home Companion*, 20 November 1943
[28] *The Home Companion*, 25 December 1943
[29] *Women's Own*, 22 June 1940
[30] *Home Chat*, 25 January 1941

[31] *Women's Own*, 6 January 1940
[32] Gardiner, Juliet. *The 1940s House*, pp 242
[33] *The Home Companion*, January-June 1946
[34] *The Home Companion*, January-June 1946
[35] *The Home Companion*, January-June 1946
[36] Marwick, Arthur, *British Society Since 1945*, Penguin 1996, p70
[37] Marwick, op. cit., p 70
[38]www2.warwick.ac.uk/fac/arts/history/undergrad/modules/hi149/lectures/lecture_notes/peoples_war
[39] *The Home Companion*, 4 May 1946
[40] *The Home Companion*, January-June 1946
[41] *Women's Own*, January-June 1947
[42] *Women's Own*, May 1947
[43] *Women's Own*, January-June 1947
[44] *Women's Own*, January-June 1947
[45] Marwick, op. cit., p 60
[46] *The Home Companion*, January-June 1946
[47] Roberts, Elizabeth, *Women and Families*, Blackwell, 1996, p29
[48] Marwick, op. cit., p69
[49] Roberts, op. cit., p29
[50] *Housewife*, June 1958
[51] *Housewife*, 1950
[52] *Women*, 23 March 1957
[53] Marwick, op. cit., p70
[54] *Women's Own*, 4 February 1950
[55] *Women's Own*, 4 February 1950
[56] *Women's Own*, 12 January 1950
[57] Roberts, op cit., p 95,96
[58] *Women's Own*, 12 January 1950
[59] Marwick, op. cit., p117
[60] Marwick, op. cit., p117
[61] *Housewife*, October 1963
[62] *Housewife*, February 1968
[63] Roberts, op.cit., p69
[64] *Women's Own*, 15 February 1964
[65] *Women and Home*, January 1965

[66] *Women's Own*, 22 June 1963
[67] Marwick, op. cit., p118
[68] www.migrationwatchuk.org/pdfs/History/6_2_Emigration_from_the_uk.pdf
[69] Roberts, op. cit., p63

8823663R00085

Printed in Great Britain
by Amazon.co.uk, Ltd.,
Marston Gate.